COPING WITH COUNSELING CRISES

FIRST AID F

BAKER BOOK HOUSE
Grand Rapids, Michigan

Reprinted 1976 by
Baker Book House Company
ISBN: 0-8010-0112-9

First printing, July 1976
Second printing, November 1976
Third printing, January 1978

PHOTOLITHOPRINTED BY CUSHING - MALLOY, INC.
ANN ARBOR, MICHIGAN, UNITED STATES OF AMERICA
1978

CONTENTS

INTRODUCTION

I delivered these lectures at Talbot Theological Seminary in October, 1975 as the Lyman Stewart Lecturer for that year. In January of 1976 they also were delivered at Capital Bible Seminary, and in February at the Seminary of the Presbyterian Church of America. Although a few emendations have been made for publication, the book is substantially the same as the lectures. However, I have added ten sample cases that may be used by students, either individually, in classes or as a part of other groups, to provide practice in applying the biblical principles of crisis counseling presented in the lectures. I hope that this addition will be of significance. Questions and directions for role play accompany each case.

My goal is to help prepare the Christian counselor to aid his people in facing the many sorts of crisis situations that they inevitably encounter in a world of sin. My prayer is that God will use this book to that end.

Jay Adams
Professor of Practical Theology
Westminster Theological Seminary
1976

CHAPTER I
FIRST AID FOR COUNSELORS

Much of the New Testament is crisis oriented. A number of the epistles, especially, were written to meet crises in the lives of individuals and churches. These crises involved all sorts of problems—heresy, apostasy, congregational division, lawsuits, disorder, death, persecution, immorality . . . . You name it, and in one form or another, you will probably find it in these letters. Christian counselors, therefore, are privileged to have the biblical resources to which to turn. Without a doubt, there is a rich lode of theoretical and practical aid available in the Bible to the crisis counselor.

Each minister of the Word, during the course of his ministry, must help others to face the many crises that unavoidably arise in a sinful world. Among other things, we must come to understand the pastoral ministry as a calling that involves helping persons in crisis. It is evident that in thoroughly equipping him for every good work,[1] God supplied an abundance of materials from which the "man of God" may abstract and marshal an impressive array of pertinent principles that is adequate to forge the practical programs and procedures that are needed to help persons in crisis. As a matter of fact, this fertile, inerrant source of help is intended to qualify him in a unique way for this work.

"Why, then, have you chosen to speak on this subject? If there is so much in the Scriptures about crisis counseling, surely by now all that could be said has been. The mine must be nearly exhausted. There must be a plethora of books on the subject and . . . ."

Excuse me. May I break in for just a moment? I agree that this is

---

[1] II Timothy 3:15-17. For further exposition of the bearing of this passage upon counseling, see *The Christian Counselor's Manual*, pp. 8, 23, 93, 158, 187, 212, 233.

precisely what one could expect (and *should* expect), but surprisingly, the facts show otherwise. To the best of my knowledge, no one has even begun to do the job; the Scriptures are still uncharted territory for the crisis counselor. Virtually nothing has been done to locate the principal deposits or to set up mining operations. The *first* word has not yet been spoken.

In this series of lectures, therefore, I should like to invite you to accompany me on trips up unexplored rivers and into virgin forests. It is inevitable, I suppose, that we shall miss much on our journey, and I should be remiss if I did not warn you of this probability. It is even altogether possible that I shall fail to show you the grandeur of some of the mightier rivers while investigating their tributaries. There are mountains to traverse, and at times the going will be hard. I cannot even tell you how far the territory extends. After all, it is a *continent* that we shall explore! Most of the way we must use the machete; there are no trails.

But, in spite of the hazards, I am convinced that the trip will prove worthwhile if only I can accomplish two objectives. First, with your help, I should like to establish a beachhead. Then, I hope to enlist some of you to become fellow explorers—and even colonists—in this vast, undeveloped wilderness. There is much to be done in this land by those who catch the vision. The opportunities are limitless.

I should say that despite these warnings, I have some solid confidence in what we are about to do. I shall try not to be a blind guide leading the blind. I have made a sufficient number of forays into the land already to assure you that we shall not get lost. But I confess that this is the first time that I have been the leader of a full-scale expedition; heretofore I have always gone alone.

But why has there been so little exploration?

I am not altogether sure. I can only suggest one or two reasons. For one thing, until recently, we have viewed the Scriptures largely from other perspectives. I do not wish to infer that these perspectives were unnecessary or unimportant; I only wish to note that our field of vision has been limited.

Another consideration should be noted: it has been only during the last few years that a growing concern about crisis counseling has emerged. That concern, to our shame, has stemmed almost exclusively from non-Christian quarters. Now, a number of Christian counselors, like Johnnie-come-latelies, have begun to show an interest too. But, that interest has produced little-or-nothing fresh, little-or-nothing distinctively Christian. Eclectically, Christian counselors again have opted for adaptations of the existing approaches that seem to be well on their way toward becoming established among non-Christian counselors. They have not bothered to do the hard work of asking, "What do the Scriptures have to say?"

In the area of counseling, as in all others, the eclectic spirit is rife. As a consequence, the highly unsatisfactory views of Lindemann and Caplan (top of the totem pole gurus in the secular crisis counseling movement) are being accepted and assimilated into the church in a totally naive fashion. This is both astounding and alarming since, in their view, human beings rigidly are caricatured as responding monolithically to grief and other crises, irrespective of the vast differences that underlie the crises and that characterize the individuals who face them. More often than not, the "grief work" (or "crisis work") theory is uncritically adopted without the slightest thought about the theological or anthropological presuppositions underlying this position. This is most disturbing, since the Lindemann grief work theory makes no room for essential distinctions between Christians and non-Christians, allows for no differences of attitudes or behavior in individuals, and views the sense of guilt, fear, anger, sorrow and other expressions of emotion as but simple states that may be handled satisfactorily by helping the counselee to progress normally through a succession of predetermined stages. Moreover, in this popular analysis, there is no place for repentance, grace, forgiveness or sanctification. The work of Christ is ignored, and what the Scriptures declare to be the fruit of the *Spirit,* crisis interventionists claim to be available apart from the work of the Spirit. How Christian counselors could propose to help people in crisis without these biblical essentials is beyond me. Lindemann's humanistic views *must* be unacceptable to the thoughtful Christian counselor.

The trip that I have planned for us is not an excursion tour that a minister might consider optional; on the contrary, it is of the greatest importance. To begin with, according to the Bible, the pastor is to be an example to the flock in all things (Titus 2:7). That means that every pastor himself must know how to meet a crisis. If he cannot, eventually he will lose credibility as a counselor. And even when *that* eventuality may be postponed, his best efforts to help others will be torpedoed by the resultant weaknesses in his own thinking and personality.

Moreover, as leader and protector of the flock, it is crucial for the pastor to know how to care for the sheep in a crisis. Otherwise, in their hour of need, he will become part of the problem rather than a part of God's solution.

It is possible, of course, for one to be able to make others aware of proper information and correct procedures and yet fail to be able to effect these in his own life. Since all counselors are sinners, to some extent this inconsistency between knowledge and practice will be present in every counseling context. No sinner—not even a redeemed one—is able to apply fully the truths of the Scriptures to his own life. Therefore, to some extent, there always will be something of a loss.

On the other hand, there are those who, because of their past training both in precept and by example, are able to meet personal crises in a manner pleasing to Christ, but, when they try to help others to face the very same sort of crises, fail. Why? They may fail because they are not able to analyze, abstract and articulate the biblical principles behind the actions by which they overcame the threats and dangers of the crises. Or, they may fail because they do not know how to raise hope in the counselee, or . . . for any other number of reasons relating to the acquisition and communication of truth. *Know how* is not the same thing as *show how.* To some extent, of course, all counselors also fail in this way. Sinners must seek perfection now, but they will attain it only in the life to come. What is true of all of the qualifications for elders in the epistles to Timothy and Titus is true also of those that pertain to counseling: they must be applied approximately, not absolutely. As Blackwood so aptly put it in the title of his last book, *The Growing Minister,* a pastor must mature continually in both knowledge and life. Yet if he knows neither how to live in this world of crisis nor how to advise others to do so, he does not possess the qualifications to be a minister of the Word. Until he can demonstrate some genuine competence in these things, he ought not be ordained to a work for which he is ill suited.

Otherwise, both he and the members of his flock will suffer the consequences. That means that you, now while you are still in Talbot Seminary, must begin to develop your ability to handle personal crises, and you must begin to learn how to help others to do so if you wish to minister to a portion of God's flock upon graduation. You need not search out crises; they will come soon enough on their own. If your professors here are anything like my colleagues at Westminster, I am sure, by their assignments and examinations, they will provide more than enough opportunities for you to face crises during your stay in this institution.

"But," you ask, "does a minister really deal with that many crisis situations? I mean, is it really worth all the effort? After all, I have a lot of Greek and Hebrew to study . . . ."

You wonder about this, possibly, because you may have known ministers who have had to counsel relatively few persons who are in crises. They may even tell you that it is *not* worth the time and effort since the opportunities to do crisis counseling are so limited. In response, let me simply suggest a few things:

First, people do not think or operate that way in other areas of life. Although there are relatively few instances in which those who are adequately trained in first aid find it necessary to perform a tracheotomy, it is, nevertheless, vital for them to know the procedure, or someone, someday whose life they might otherwise have saved may die of suffocation. Let us suppose, for the sake of the argument, that a given minister receives only a half dozen or so phone calls from persons threatening suicide during his entire ministry. Is it not still important for him to know what to do when such a call comes? Or, can he simply write off those six persons as "a limited number of cases?" May he rationalize by saying "After all, I shall preach to hundreds, perhaps even thousands, so I must concentrate all of my attention on preaching?" Any such attitude falls far short of the spirit of the Good Shepherd who not only feeds the ninety-nine sheep at hand but also seeks the hundredth that is lost.

But then, if a minister tells you that he has relatively few crisis counseling cases, in most instances (if he has been in the pastorate for any significant length of time), you can begin to question whether that man has an effective ministry to his people. There is no dearth of crises and no lack of persons—even Christian persons—who are failing to meet them God's way. Why, then, do those sheep to whom he ministers not seek him out more often? In contrast, *truly* ministering pastors tell of the overwhelming number of such cases that they see.[2]

Particular circumstances, in certain situations, may (of course) limit the number of crisis cases that a minister may encounter for reasons not attributable to him. But, in general, it may be said with assurance that the effective pastor is at least as deeply involved in crisis counseling as anyone else in any other profession, and much more fully than most.

Simply for the sake of the many who experience crises in their marriage and families, and in order to minister well to the sick and dying, the pastor should find a study of biblical principles and practices pertinent to crisis counseling essential. You can be certain that every hour you spend increasing your knowledge and developing the skills involved in crisis counseling will at length prove profitable.

Since it should not be necessary to extend the present argument further, I shall make two additional responses briskly, then move on. Some pastors are so unacquainted with the particular features and peculiarities of the crisis situation that they don't recognize a crisis when they see one. These same men often are the ones who are so insensitive to the needs of their people that they fail to discern the symptoms of persons going through a crisis. Secondly, there are some pastors, I am afraid, who do not want to recognize a crisis. Like the priest and Levite, they close their eyes and walk by. They try not to become involved either out of laziness or fear. Crisis counseling is hard work, and it runs risks. It takes both effort and time, and requires courage and wisdom.

That fact leads to a discussion of the counselor himself. In the lectures that follow we shall have occasion to consider the crisis situation and the person in crisis. We must not forget the counselor.

[2]In response to a student questionnaire by students at Westminster in 1973, 13 out of 35 ministers said that 50% of their counseling was crisis counseling. The rest estimated that crisis counseling constituted anywhere from 5% - 90% of their counseling.

We have just said that he must be a man of wisdom and courage. To that let me add the need for commitment and concern.

By concern, I mean something more than sympathy. Concern is not *only* weeping with those who weep—as essential as that may be—but also the willingness to help another to do something about his problems. Sympathy, too often, means "sympathetic *agreement.*" But that sort of expression of solidarity with the sufferer goes too far, since seeing a crisis only as the counselee does, in fact, precludes the possibility of helping him. If the counselee is perplexed it may make him feel better temporarily if you share his perplexity, but sharing it will not help him out of it. If he has lost hope, acknowledging the hopelessness of his situation may be comforting for a time, but it will not restore hope. The counselor must be able to enter into the counselee's problem, but he must be able to get beyond it as well. If he is merely caught up in it, he too will be disabled by it. Because he has the Scriptures, he need not stop with the problem. He may move quickly along the biblical path that leads out of it.

Scriptural concern, therefore, is not the expression of sympathetic agreement; rather, it is the expression of sympathetic *disagreement.* It is only by *countering* perplexity, and hopelessness, and depression, and temper, and fear with biblical alternatives that the counselor maintains his integrity as such. The Christian counselor is not a neighbor who holds pity parties on the phone each afternoon; he is a man with a biblical alternative.

But the counselor must have wisdom in order to manifest the right kind of concern. It takes wisdom, for instance, to maintain a balance between sympathy and disagreement. He must know how deeply to allow himself to enter into the counselee's situation while, at the same time, assuming a stance over against the counselee's present helpless position. To see the problem only as the counselee does is not merely a matter of abandoning one's place as a counselor; of far greater import is the fact that when he does so, the counselor misrepresents God. As a Christian counselor, he is required to know and articulate God's solution. Therefore, when he fails to do this, the counselee is led to believe that God does not have an answer to his problem. There is always *something* that can be done, even if it is to take the first step toward the biblical solution. Frequently, it will involve a change in the attitude and responses of the counselee. But whatever it may be, the Christian counselor must hold the conviction that in some way biblical help *will make a difference*. No one ever needs to go away from Christian counseling the same. If he has been confronted with the Word of God, he can be different in some way, that day.

It is in learning the facts of the crisis situation, in evaluating them biblically, and in discovering the biblical responses required by them that the Christian counselor must develop knowledge and skill. It is in confronting the counselee with these as an alternative to his present stance that he will need wisdom and courage.

Sympathetic agreement takes no courage and calls for little wisdom; sympathetic disagreement demands both. It is not easy to tell a depressed woman that she must get off the couch and get to work, that she must stop feeling sorry for herself, and that she must confess and forsake any other sin in her life. To tell an irate husband whose wife has given notice that she plans to leave him that his resentment is sin and needs to be abandoned may not be popular, but it may be the only way for him to handle the tragedy in a manner that is pleasing to God. And, incidentally, if he does, that change in him will probably do more to persuade her to reconsider than anything else he could do. Certainly, allowing him to storm about the study, or permitting him to excoriate his wife in bitter language solves no problems. Sympathetic *disagreement* calls for settling him down and confronting him with his own sin first. That type of concern requires the courage to confront.

Now, on balance, I must hasten to say that sympathetic disagreement is quite a different approach from that which was taken by the counselors who confronted Job. Doubtless, their breed did not die quickly; today, we meet their representatives frequently. Like Job's friends, they fancy themselves as being quite biblical. Yet it is they who bring biblical confrontation into disrepute. People are constantly confusing *their* approach with the biblical one. It is important, therefore to take time to distinguish between the two.

When Job's friends came to offer counsel, they surely disagreed— of that there can be no question. There was confrontation—of *that* the record leaves no doubt. Since they are called "friends," there is even a likelihood that there was a measure of concern. But what

Job's friends lacked was sympathy, not the sentimental sort that could never ride side-by-side with disagreement and confrontation, but the sort of sympathetic concern that includes these and combines them with a full analysis of the situation and a loving belief in the word of the counselee. Presumably they had the capacity for neither; thus they failed to provide the help that Job needed. The Christian crisis counselor must excel precisely in the three things they failed to do:

1. First, they came with preconceived notions about the cause of Job's problem. As a result, they failed to gather the data that might have led to a true analysis of the situation.

2. Secondly, they refused to listen to Job when he protested that their assumptions and (therefore) their conclusions were wrong. They failed to follow the biblical maxim that leads to successful counseling: "love believes all things." In love, the biblical counselor doubts the word of the counselee *only when the facts demand that he do so.*

3. Like many modern counselors, Job's friends began with their own assumptions and doubted that Job was telling the truth. Because of these two fundamental errors, they also fell into a third: Job's counselors failed to uncover Job's real problem and, therefore, could not help him with it. By focusing their attention upon supposed prior failures in Job's life that they considered to be the cause of Job's crisis, they missed entirely the meaning and depth of his true struggle. This is tragic since, as the record shows, Job *needed* the help that they might have provided. Instead of providing help, they succeeded only in aggravating the situation. Job was not responsible for the crisis, as they supposed, but God held him responsible for how he would handle it.[3] The heavenly discussion between God and Satan focused, you will remember, upon *this* issue: "What will Job do when trouble comes?" But the problem as these would-be-counselors saw it was, "What has Job done to bring this crisis upon himself?" They confronted him—but at the wrong point. The real question was "How will Job face a crisis?"

[3]Counselors must remember that this is often so. The daughter of a drunkard who beats her and fails to provide for her may not be responsible for this situation, but she is responsible for handling it God's way.

So, from one perspective, a good crisis counselor is one who has enough courageous concern to take a different and more biblical view of the crisis than the counselee, yet he will always reach his conclusions in the matter, by examination of carefully collected data. Unlike Job's friends, he will work hard to discover all of the dimensions of the problem. Then, and only then, out of concern, he will take a biblical stance toward it, no matter how sharply this may require him to disagree with the counselee's conclusions.

Now, let me attempt to define a crisis. One dictionary says that it is a stage in a sequence of events at which the trend of all future events is determined. Although that definition seems a bit overly dramatic for some crises, nevertheless from one viewpoint it certainly seems to describe Job's situation reasonably well. The glaring fault in this definition, from the Christian perspective, is its uniformitarianism or determinism—i.e., its failure to take God into account. The same dictionary further defines a crisis as a "turning point" and "a point at which a decisive change occurs." I am not in the habit of quoting the dictionary to prove points, since it rarely does that. However, in these definitions you will notice that there is more than one way to speak about a crisis. It is that fact that I want to make. A crisis is described either as a point in time at which something decisive occurs (or is about to occur), or as a condition, state or critical stage of instability leading to a decisive change. Since otherwise there might be confusion, I want you to understand that in these lectures I shall use the word to refer to both the state and the turning point. Putting the two together, we may say that a crisis is any situation into which God has led the counselee that either now or later demands decisive action that will have significant consequences. A crisis requires change.

And, while we are at it, let me say too that it is important to go beyond the dictionary and make a further distinction: a crisis may be either real or imagined. The emotional impact upon the counselee will be just as real and just as powerful even if the crisis is only imagined. If he is told convincingly that he has cancer, whether the fact is true or false, his emotional response will be exactly the same. When discussing crisis counseling, therefore, we may speak not only of the person in the crisis, but also of *the crisis in the person*. That means that counseling may be just as essential in an imaginary crisis as in a real one. Indeed, the problem may be even greater, and the counselor may need to make an *exhaustive* analysis of the situation in order to be able to discover and convince the counselee of the imaginary nature of the supposed crisis.

A crisis, then, is any circumstance to which a person senses a need to respond, in which he believes that his response may have life-shaking effects.

Fundamentally, there are three elements to be considered in every crisis:

1. The crisis situation (real or imagined),

2. The individual who is in crisis, and

3. The response that he must make to the crisis issues.

The counselor must be concerned with each of these elements. In each crisis he will find it helpful to simplify his task by breaking it down into these elements. Immediately, when he does so, he may discover that he needs to *focus* his attention upon one or more elements. If, for instance, the attitude of the individual toward God is proper, and if he possesses adequate resources otherwise, the counselor's task may be reduced to analyzing the crisis situation and helping him to determine how to respond to it. If, on the other hand, the counselee understands the crisis well enough, knows what God wants him to do and how to do it, but refuses to do so, the counselor must focus upon the person, rather than upon the situation or the decision. So, you can see how helpful it can be to divide a crisis into these three elements.

Each of these elements must be considered fully in relationship to the obligations and the promises of God. The Christian counselor seeks to bring scriptural aid to the counselee in one or more of these three areas. Full aid, i.e., aid in all three areas, involves helping the counselee:

1. To make a biblical *analysis* of the crisis situation,

2. To take a personal *inventory* of his state, attitudes, behavior and resources, and

3. To follow biblical *directions* in responding to the issues in the crisis situation.

Thus, the framework for crisis counseling consists of three critical factors corresponding to the three elements in the crisis. Those factors are:

Analysis, Inventory and Direction

For a counselor to analyze a situation, take the inventory of the state and resources of a counselee, and be able to give biblical direction about the proper response to a crisis, he must acquire the knowledge and skills necessary to do so. During each of the next three lectures I shall consider one of these three factors with a view to helping you become acquainted with some of that knowledge. Skills, and the wisdom with which to exercise them, must come from the prayerful application and use of this knowledge.

"But," you may ask, "how did you arrive at the three elements of which you speak?" That is a fair question to which I have time to address myself only briefly. Let me say right away that this framework has emerged from the study of a number of crisis situations in the Scriptures. In each of these situations these three elements frequently appear as matters of concern. I do not claim that they all are present in every situation, nor am I sure that we would all agree about labeling all of the situations considered, "crises." Moreover, that there may be other elements that should be isolated and included in this framework, is altogether possible. And, finally, that others might prefer to breakdown the total crisis context quite differently—and perhaps more accurately—is not unlikely. Therefore, let me say as plainly as possible that while I think that this framework is biblical and (therefore) useful, I do not say that it is as fully biblical or as fully useful as another might be. But at present it is the only one that I have.

To support my contention that there is biblical support for this framework let us consider a passage or two in which a crisis is met in a thoroughly biblical fashion.

The Book of III John was written by the apostle to Gaius as a stopgap measure to help him to handle a crisis in a manner pleasing to Christ. The congregation to which Gaius belonged was in jeopardy as the result of the pride and ambition of Diotrophes, who (in all likelihood) was the pastor of the church. Diotrophes had refused to show hospitality to travelling missionaries whom John had sent forth to preach the gospel on the basis of his apostolic authority. Because he did not wish to share the limelight with them, Diotrophes not only rejected the missionaries himself, but forbade his members to show them hospitality upon pain of excommunication. Gaius had warmly received the missionaries, and presumably had been thrown out of the church. As he sat outside on the curb scratching his head, he wondered "Did I do the right thing or not?"

When he learned of these affairs, John wrote to Diotrophes about his sinful actions, but instead of repentance and compliance, he received a slanderous rebuff. It was not a personal matter with John; the problem was that in rejecting his apostolic authority Diotrophes was rejecting the authority of Jesus Christ. Now, in this letter to Gaius John says that he plans to come and handle the matter personally as soon as he can. But, meanwhile on a single sheet of papyrus John penned this letter and shot it off to Gaius in order to help him face the crisis in his life and in the church.

We shall have occasion to return to this crisis situation later on, but for the moment, notice how fully all three elements appear. John completely analyzes the situation, carefully assesses Gaius' attitudes, actions and resources in relationship to it, and clearly directs him in the responses that are proper to make. All three elements—the crisis situation, the individual in crisis, and the proper response to the crisis—figure prominently in the letter.

Because he was an apostle, writing Scripture, John did not need to base his counsel directly upon Scripture passages. Perhaps, for this reason it would be appropriate to consider next the letter of Jude. Jude also writes by divine inspiration, but makes no personal claims to apostolic authority. He more nearly approaches our context then. In the crisis of which he wrote, we see the same three elements once again. Dropping his reed in the middle of a sentence, Jude crumbled up the sheet of papyrus upon which he had been writing, took up another and addressed himself to the startling news that had just reached him. His words . . . "it became urgently necessary to write at once and appeal to you to join the struggle in defense of the faith that God entrusted to his people once and for all" (v.3), plainly reveal the crisis nature of the situation about which he wrote.

There is neither time nor space to discuss the letter in depth but upon study and reflection I think you will see those same three elements and those same three counselor responses protruding. Jude carefully analyzes what is happening, in terms of Peter's second letter. In the strictest sense of the word, he makes a *biblical analysis* of the situation. Then, using Peter and data from other biblical sources, he discusses the state of the congregation, pointing out the personal and congregational resources that God has provided for such contingencies, and finally, he urges decisive concrete action upon his readers.

If I were to give a subtitle to these lectures, it would be something like "First Aid for Christian Counselors." In a medical crisis, one can not do everything immediately; often all he can do is give *first* aid. Yet that is important. We have all been made newly aware of the vital nature of that initial aid by the TV program, "Emergency." Of course, more sophisticated help—in greater depth—is given later in the hospital.

Similarly, important things can be accomplished in crisis counseling; but not everything. It is only during the period of more regularized counseling that many other things can be done. This should be kept in mind, so that not too much will be expected from crisis counseling. So long as the emergency element prevails, counseling must be limited to crisis approaches. So, one of the goals of crisis counseling always will be to eliminate the elements of urgency and emergency in order to allow for the fuller, and the more sophisticated approaches of pastoral counseling.

In summing up, let me push the First Aid analogy a bit. If a crisis consists of a crisis situation, a person in crisis and decisive responses that must be made to resolve it, and if good crisis counseling addresses itself to these three elements by making an *analysis* of the situation, taking an *inventory* of the attitudes, actions and resources of the person in crisis in order to give *direction* to the counselee about the biblical responses required, then in the simple mnemonic, A-I-D (Analysis, Inventory, Direction) you have it. Just think of crisis counseling as a sort of First *Aid* and in days to come that little three letter word may come to your aid as you endeavor to aid another!

CHAPTER II

ANALYSIS

It is impossible to escape all crises in a world of sin. In the providence of God, for His sovereign purposes, crises come. Some we bring upon ourselves; others (as in the case of Job) come through no fault of our own. Some crises are simple and straightforward: "Shall I divorce my husband for incompatibility?" Others, are far more complex: "My whole life has suddenly caved in—my hopes, my values, my goals—everything, and I don't know where to turn or what to do." Some crises are imagined; some real. Some are contrived (in order to avoid responsibility or to manipulate others); many are not.

Distinctions like these are arrived at by means of *analysis* , and constitute one aspect of the work of analysis. Apart from such work, it is difficult for the counselor even to *begin* to help a person in crisis, since he must determine the nature of the crisis situation in biblical terms before he can develop a scriptural strategy with which to meet it. If the crisis is contrived or imaginary, to treat it merely as if it were legitimate or real would be the height of folly. In my last lecture, I suggested that John and Jude had first fully analyzed the crises about which they wrote. The fundamental place of analysis, therefore, should be obvious. Everything else in crisis counseling depends upon it.

When Paul faced the council in Jerusalem, it was through analysis of the speaking situation that he arrived at the decision to explain his mission in the terms that he chose—terms true enough, but *also,* terms that he knew would divide his accusers into two camps.[1] Strategy was based upon analysis. In the messages of the risen Christ to the seven churches (some of which were in a crisis or were about to face one) the same procedure is evident: first, there is a summary of

[1]Acts 23:6.

the results of Christ's analysis, introduced in each case by the phrase
"I know " ("I know where you dwell" . . . , "I know your
tribulation." "I know your deeds."); then counsel is given that grows
out of and is appropriate to that analysis. *This,* is the sort of thing
that I am talking about; until with Jesus the counselor can say "I
know . . . ," he is not ready to offer help. To call for an analysis of
each crisis, therefore, simply means to ask seriously, and to answer
thoroughly out of careful study of the particular situation, "What
sort of crisis is it that my counselee is facing?"

There is more to analysis than that, as we shall see soon, but
before looking into other apsects of the question, let me make a
remark or two about a connected issue of some importance.

Because it is not possible to avoid all crises, we must learn to deal
with them. But few persons have ever been taught how to do so. Ask
yourself, has anyone ever taught *you*? Well, that is one reason why
there is such a need for crisis counseling today.

C. S. Lewis opened his book, *A Grief Observed,* with these
plaintive words: "No one ever told me . . . ." Doubtless, if someone
had more adequately prepared him for the crisis of grief about which
he wrote, he would have been able to handle it in a better manner
than he did. Pastors must learn to help the members of their
congregations *preventively* by preparing them for crises. It is
foolish—not to say tragic—to wait until a person has come unglued
in a crisis to begin giving instruction. The pastor, if he is a faithful
shepherd of the sheep, will not be content to lock the door after the
sheep has wandered out. Christian ministers always should be
concerned to hang the traffic light at the corner *before* someone is
killed in a bloody accident.

Yet, at present, there is neither enough remedial work being done
by Christians, nor anywhere near enough preventive effort. We are
woefully deficient in both. Since I cannot discuss preventive
measures as such in these lectures, I wish to underscore the need for
them by these few brief comments, and urge each of you to give
further thought on your own to the matter. The members of your
congregations in years to come will thank God for your ministry if
you make the effort to teach them how to handle a crisis before it
comes. Young married couples should be helped to discuss grief

before losing their parents. Teenagers, who often live from one crisis till the next, must learn *as preteens* how to avoid bringing on crises that are unnecessary and how to handle the many jolting boy/girl experiences that they cannot avoid.

But it is not only because I want to urge you to think through preventive crisis instruction on your own that I mention the subject. It should also be obvious as we go on, that many of the same principles that pertain to counseling someone who is already in a crisis, apply equally as well to preparing for a crisis and meeting it on one's own, before God, by His help, and without the assistance of a human counselor.

At times it might be useful not only to teach the biblical principles for handling crises, but also to dramatize these through acting out some typical crisis situations. Well . . . that is all that I can say now about preventive measures. But remember, as we proceed, in this lecture (as well as in those that follow) to keep this matter on the front of the shelf where you can get your hands on it easily from time to time.

Now, let us return to the question of analysis, the A in AID. First, let me be clear about how the word is being used. Whenever I speak of the analysis of a crisis, I use the word to refer to the process of breaking apart the situation into its constituent elements. By putting it that way I imply that:

1. Every crisis has parts, aspects or elements that, for purposes of understanding and solution, can be separated in *some* sense.

2. It is an error to impose an artificial structure upon the crisis situation so that each and every crisis is dissected in the same way. Like a diamond, each crisis must be studied individually to determine the peculiar points at which it ought to be cut. This decision comes from within; it is not imposed from without. The nature of each crisis itself, like the nature of the diamond, always must dictate where the chisel is to be placed.

In order to handle crises successfully, the counselor must divide the whole into its parts—or at least some of its parts. It may be important to divide and even subdivide more fully in some areas than in others. For instance, Jude in writing to one faction of the church, divides them from at least two others. In addition to his readers, there are the heretics who have invaded the church, and those who have been influenced by them. While the heretics are lumped together, in his analysis the persons who were being caught up in the heresy are not. Instead, Jude subdivides this group into three classes, each having a distinct relationship to the heretics and to their false teaching. By distinguishing between them, he is able to recommend specific and individualized help that is appropriate to each class: "have mercy on some who are doubting; save others,— snatching them out of the fire; and on some have mercy with fear, hating even the garment polluted by the flesh" (22,23).

Crises, then, usually come as wholes, not in parts, and virtually scream for analysis (or, as we are now thinking of it, *division*). Frequently, it is this very wholeness that constitutes the crisis element in the situation: "The woods are too vast, too dark, too tangled. What shall I do?" Such complaints are the constant cry of persons who need help in facing crisis situations. In such cases, taking the crisis apart, setting up a biblical plan for dealing with each element in some order according to a schedule, and beginning to focus upon the first element right away, may be exactly what the counselee needs to solve his problem.

But, how can I determine when this need for division is one of the factors that is fundamental?"

You will probably need to make an analysis of the situation in almost every instance anyway simply to sort things out, to know where to begin your counseling. So, the question is not as important as at first it might seem. If in the process of sorting out, the counselee comes alive, begins to participate in the process himself and starts to see light, keep working at it together and you may discover that principally what he needed was the handle on the problem that you have now given to him. Surely that is much of what the New Testament is all about, when (as in James) Christians undergoing temptation are shown that God cannot be blamed for their temptation, but that they must look at their own evil desires, or when (as in II Peter) the scoffer's charge of slowness in keeping a promise is distinguished from the longsuffering of God by which He patiently waits till the last one of His elect comes to faith.

But, to answer your question more specifically, you can almost be certain that your counselee needs to divide and distinguish the things that differ, or that he needs to take on a part rather than the whole:

1. *When he continually speaks about the enormity of the crisis.* Whenever he expresses his problem in language like "This is too much," or "This is more than I can take," or "How will I ever get all of this done?" you may begin to suspect that you have a situation that needs division into its parts. He is overwhelmed by the whole. If he says "I've bitten off more than I can chew," why not agree and help him to slice up the whole into chewable bite size portions?

2. *When he is confused over the complexity of the crisis.* Language denoting a tangled, can-of-worms situation about which the counselee expresses confusion also gives a clue: "I just get all confused when I try to think about it" or "I just don't know where to begin."

3. *When he is worried about having to do more than is realistic on a given day.* This is expressed in language taking the form of "But, what will I do if . . . ? The what-if formula connected to strong emotion is almost always indicative of worry. In such cases, the counselor must help the counselee to learn how to take apart his problems each day and allocate those that belong to the present a place on today's schedule; the rest must be rescheduled for consideration in the future. Christ once said, when speaking of worry:

Do not worry about tomorrow . . . . Each day has enough trouble of its own (Mt. 6:34).

The biblical word for worry—interestingly enough—means to "separate, divide or take apart." The counselor, therefore, must help the counselee to take apart the situation, before the situation takes him apart.

4. *When a counselee complains of unfairness.* In such cases he fails to distinguish human responsibility from divine sovereignty. Language like "Why did *this* have to happen?" or "Everything always happens to *me* "or "Joe isn't even a

Christian, and yet *he* doesn't suffer like this" is indicative of the sort of difficulty that James, Peter and the Psalmist, who keeps warning us not to fret over the fortunes of the unbeliever, were confronting. The irresponsibilities of scoffers and their way of thinking must be distinguished from God's providence. One's own evil desires must be sorted out from God's testings, and the temporal prosperity of the wicked must *not* be contrasted with the temporal suffering of the believer, but the temporal condition of each must be compared with the eternal state of each.

In all of these instances, in one way or another, various elements in the situation need to be sorted out. And it is this kind of basic analysis of the whole—in which constituent elements are isolated for comparison and contrast, or for proper scheduling, or for easier understanding and handling—that must come first. Often, as I have said, such analysis *itself* will do much to resolve a crisis.

Let's take a typical crisis situation in which it is this approach that makes the difference.

I'm ruined. I'm at the end of my rope. All of the chickens have come home to roost. I am a financial disaster! I'll lose my house . . . .Pastor, what can I do?

Where does the counselor begin? He asks, "Gary, how much do you owe?" In response, Gary says "I don't know; I just don't know. But it is more than I can handle—I know that!"

Immediately, a good counselor would be suspicious. How could Gary be so concerned about financial ruin when he cannot even substantiate it? Something is wrong. The first task this counselor needs to accomplish is to *get the facts*. He must separate emotion from reality, generalizations from specifics. Consequently, he will try to discover how much is owed to whom for what, what Gary's financial resources actually are, and which creditors (if any) are breathing down his neck. He will also try to discover what precipitated the crisis. When an analysis of the situation is in, the facts can be sorted out and a program can be designed to meet the problem. The likelihood is, as in Gary's case, that once doing so, the answer will be readily apparent. In many instances, ruin is the last word by which the situation now can be described. The "ruinous" or "crisis" element was introduced by *Gary* who allowed his obligations to pile up without keeping records, etc. Reintroducing the element of organization as an obligation of faith, it may be achieved first by sorting out the facts and dividing the urgent from the less urgent, and then by planning accordingly. This often makes the difference. But notice, analysis had to come first.

Now, let us turn to a different matter. We have said that a crisis is a situation in which action leading to serious consequences is required. That is one way to look at it. But you will recall that I criticized the dictionary definition because it left God out. The Christian counselor must not do that. Indeed, that is precisely what makes his counsel unique; he will analyze the situation from a biblical (that is, from a theistic) point of view.

God is sovereign. No matter how bad the crisis may appear to be, it is never beyond His ability to resolve. And furthermore, neither is it beyond God's purview or His concern. Every hair on the counselee's head is numbered. He works *all* things together for *good* to those who love Him; who are called according to His purposes. Even this crisis, then, is a part of God's sovereign purpose. The time will come when the Christian will see *how* it was all for his benefit— but that time is usually on the *lee* side of the crisis. That is why it is so easy to leave God out of the picture, and that is why the counselor must make every effort to reintroduce Him. By bringing God into the picture, I do not refer to reading a Scripture verse or two, with prayer. That is necessary. But too often, the way in which the Scriptures and prayer are brought into the picture is quite superficial. They do not intrude so dynamically that the entire crisis situation must be re-evaluated; rather, they merely are tacked on. But God cannot be tacked on. He will not allow Himself to be a party to an essentially humanistic analysis of the circumstances. Rather, He must be seen to be the most basic, the most vital, the most dramatic and the most hopeful element in the situation.

One of the principal reasons why Christian counselees freeze before a crisis is because they view it in essentially the same way that an unbeliever might—apart from God and His purpose. The counselor's task is to relate God *fully* to the crisis. It is crucial for him to restructure the entire picture as one in which God is at work achieving His purposes for the blessing of His own, for the furtherance of the gospel and for the honor of His Son. To do this so profoundly *changes* the crisis that it takes on an entirely new dimension. It becomes a crisis *in which God is involved.*

That is what Paul did for his Philippian readers when, in answer to their perplexed inquiries about why the greatest missionary of all had been shelved by imprisonment in Rome, he wrote:

> My circumstances have turned out for the greater progress of the gospel (Philips 1:12).

In the verses that follow, he showed them how imprisonment had occasioned an opportunity to evangelize many men among the Praetorian guard, how many other brethren were now coming forth to proclaim Christ with a new boldness, and how he was about to be afforded the opportunity to present the gospel to Caesar himself. If Paul, like his readers, had failed to see the sovereign purpose of God at work in his imprisonment, he could have looked on the imprisonment only as a terrible tragedy. He might have doubted either the wisdom of God or His power to control all things. And, doubtless, in such a frame of mind, he would have lost his witness to the guards, failed to stimulate other Christians to proclaim Christ, and wavered in his witness before the emperor of the world. Because he so firmly believed that God *was* involved in the crisis, he was able to look for and work toward the outcomes that when he wrote the letter, he was able to share with the church at Philippi.

I shall say more about God's place in a crisis in another lecture, but before I leave it, I wish to make two vital points about the effect of such a radical Christian theistic analysis of a crisis situation—the first is this:

> To acknowledge God as sovereign over the crisis *limits* it.

Don't miss this point. God is in control. The crisis is not a broken thermometer—with bits of mercury irretrievably going everywhere. God made the mercury and He knows where every little bead is. If He wills, He can gather them all together into one lump again.

Therefore, the counselee's thoughts and language can be and must be changed; the situation is neither "hopeless" nor "impossible." It is neither "too much" for him nor "out of control." The One who said "I will be with you till the end of the age" is here; Christ is in the crisis. Therefore, it is *limited* —limited to His purposes, to serve His ends, controlled at every point by His power. The crisis is in God's hands; it will not continue a fraction of a second longer than He wills, nor will it extend a millimeter beyond the limits of His design.

Secondly, if God is in the crisis: There is *meaning* to it all.

The vicissitudes of life are not merely tragic moments of absurd episodes in the saga of human existence. There is purpose, meaning, *joy* in the midst of pain and sorrow. If there is meaning, the believer can rest on that, he can search it out insofar as it is possible in this life, and he even can participate in bringing it about. In short, if God is involved in the crisis, he can be too. Life is not just a crazy, dirty, sordid, meaningless mess from which one ultimately shrinks; no! There is something worthwhile, something exciting, something adventurous, something *holy* in it—God is in life, doing inscrutable, magnificent things that *some* day we shall understand fully. So with a sense of basic joy and anticipation we can slave, and serve, and sweat, and soil our hands—because there is a point to it all: God is in the crisis!

So analysis not only means *slicing up* the crisis into its fundamental elements to see what it is made of, and isolating and identifying these more manageable pieces for study and control; it is a matter of *sizing up* the crisis as well. Analysis involves seeing the situation for what it actually is—an incident in the plan of God, bounded on all sides by His purposes and love.

We have seen that since God is in the crisis, all language and thought that speak of the crisis as if it were beyond limits ("it's too much," "impossible," and so on) are wrong. It is wrong not merely because it is inaccurate; it is wrong because (like the dictionary definition) it is *pagan* to speak that way. But when we size up a crisis *biblically* we discover that it is of *limited* extent; it is limited by God's will. As Job discovered it can achieve only His purposes—and nothing more.

Further, consider this important fact: every crisis is limited by the faithfulness of God to his children—We read:

> There is no trial that has overtaken you but what is common to man, and God is faithful, who will not allow you to be tested beyond that which you are able to bear, but (with the test) also

will provide the way out of it, that you may be able to bear it (I Cor. 10:13).

God promises three encouraging things:

1. No trial is unique. Others have gone through it successfully before you. There is hope and responsibility in that.

2. Every trial is uniquely fitted to each Christian. None *exceeds* his ability to bear— *if* he handles it God's way. Again, there is hope and responsibility in *that*.

3. God will deliver His children from the trial. It will not continue on and on; there will be a way out—by rescue from it, change within it or solutions to it. The promise of this verse means that God's presence in the crisis assures us that it is limited to what each believer can endure and handle successfully. And note, God backs up this promise by His faithfulness; that means it no more can fail, than His faithfulness can fail. There is hope and responsibility in that.

Lastly, the presence of God in a crisis means that there is adequate strength and wisdom available to meet the crisis. When Paul wrote "I can do all things through Christ who strengthens me" (Philippians 4:13), he was not penning pious platitudes. He wrote those words in a crisis; he was speaking about his experience of Christ's faithfulness in other crises, to people who had seen a demonstration of the fact in still another crisis. When this letter from prision was read in the Philippian church, there was present a jailer who must have remembered the manifestation of Christ's strength in Paul during a previous imprisonment. No, these ae not the words of an untried seminarian, still wet behind the ears; this is the apostle Paul speaking. In the midst of every crisis, Christ had proven Himself faithful in supplying the strength to do everything that He requires.

This is a biblical analysis of a crisis; one that—in whatever ways he can—the counselor must convey to the counselee: the crisis is limited by the presence of God. He limits its power, its scope, its purpose. The crisis has meaning; it is part of the plan of God. Therefore, not only can it be faced and met successfully by His strength, but the counselee can participate in it as part of God's inscrutable goodness toward him.

Probably, it is most important for the counselor to understand and believe this himself. Whether or not he is able to articulate every aspect of the biblical perspective, the counselor *will* convey his attitudes. If he understands and accepts this biblical viewpoint, the two critical ingredients of hope and responsibility will come through. And that is exactly what the counselee needs in the analysis of the problems that he must solve.

Enough for the theological and presuppositional stance toward a crisis. Let's turn, in the time that remains, to a *practical* approach to analysis.

In analyzing any crisis situation, the counselor must work with facts. He cannot work with abstractions and theories, or with guesses and suppositions; he must become concrete: just what is it that the counselee faces? Is the crisis what he *thinks* it is, or something else? Is it as serious as he suspects or even more so? How can these, and a dozen other questions like them, be answered? Only the facts, gathered, reinterpreted, assessed, sorted out and programmed for action, in a manner that is in full accord with the Scriptures, can answer these questions. There is no other way to reach satisfying solutions than through the hard work of dealing with facts. Analysis means, in the *final* analysis, doing whatever is biblically legitimate to get a *grasp* on the facts.

I have mentioned five activities that will help the counselor (and through him, the counselee) to get a biblical grasp of the facts. They are: gathering facts, reinterpreting facts, assessing facts, sorting out facts and programming facts. Let's take a quick look at each activity to understand it, in a way that will enable us to get down to the facts and apply this approach to any crisis situation.

First, it is essential to gather the facts about the situation. Contrary to counseling theories that stress the person and the expression of his feelings, and ignore the situation in which he is involved, biblical counseling is always concerned about both. Indeed, it is impossible to express meaningful concern about the person without becoming involved in his predicament. The facts of his problem are important. Since I have discussed this matter in detail elsewhere,[1] I shall do no more than remind you of this crucial difference today. Again, in my book, *The Christian Counselor's Manual,* I devoted more than one chapter to the discussion of data gathering. Since so much has been said already about this question, I shall make but one or two additional observations.

To begin with, data gathering in a *crisis* may be more difficult than at other times, particularly if the person in crisis is in a state of high emotional excitement, or if the data must be gathered quickly. Very seldom will it be possible to collect information by means of a Personal Data Inventory or some equivalent data-gathering instrument. Often, the amount of data that it is possible to obtain will be far less than at other times. Since early returns on any dramatic event tend to be confused and inaccurate, much of what is gathered ought to be held tentatively. Sometimes, if he is in shock, or if he is overwhelmed, the person in crisis cannot be relied upon to give adequate, accurate information in logical sequence, and the counselor may find it necessary to interview other involved persons in more depth. So, it is clear that in order to get a satisfactory grasp of the facts in a crisis, more often than he might like, the counselor must accommodate his normal process of data gathering in flexible and creative ways. But, note, the key word here is *adapt*; I did not say *abandon*. The same principles of data gathering still pertain.

"Concretely," you ask, "what are some ways of adapting?" Let me be specific. For one thing, the more highly emotional the person in crisis may be, the more structured the counselor's approach must be. If, for instance, the counselee is pouring forth all sorts of information in disconnected bursts, he cannot be depended upon to structure the process himself. That means that the counselor must be definite and sure about what he wants to know.

Closely related to the definiteness of the counselor, who must assume the proper sort of take-charge attitude in a crisis where there is no structure evident, is the matter of selectivity. Not everything one would like to know can be obtained readily. The materials sought must be determined by the counselor, therefore, through a much more narrowly-oriented approach that settles for less

[1] *Competent To Counsel.*

information in lesser detail. That means that in approaching the counselee in the crisis situation, the counselor must know what he wants and go right after it without any preliminaries or any further ado. While most of the information on the Personal Data Inventory will not be appropriate, he (for instance) will probably want to ask what we have called, the three basics: What happened?, What have you done about it so far?, and What do you want me to do?" Yet even here, he may find it necessary to settle for answers that are spotty and partial—answers that would never do in a more relaxed or slower moving counseling context.

But since it is important for the counselor to be clear about what to ask, so that he can structure the data gathering process in the most efficient way, let me further suggest that his questioning focus upon three areas:

1. *The persons involved in the crisis.* What are they? In what ways are they involved? Are there others besides those who are immediately apparent to the counselee? The focus on persons is critical. Few counseling crises have only to do with things. The most emotionally-laden aspect of the crisis is the personal element. Even financial reverses become crises *only* because of the personal implications of the loss. And, while we are discussing this area, let me remind you again to be sure that the counselee has a clear view of *the* person and his altogether critical role in the crisis.

2. *The relationship of the counselee to each person who is involved, and what his responsibility is to each.* Does he owe money? Must he seek someone's forgiveness? Has someone slandered his name?

3. *The issues that have emerged already, or that are likely to emerge very soon.* What are they? Of what sorts? etc.

So, three all-important areas of data gathering, then, are: the *persons* who, directly or indirectly, are involved in the crisis, the *relationship and responsibilities* that the counselee bears to each, and the *issues* that need to be resolved. And, into each of these areas the three basic questions can be introduced: What happened to you and to any other persons who might have been involved?, What have you done about the actions of any of these persons?, What do you want me to do about them? Or, take the second area: What happened to your relationship to each of these persons? And what are your responsibilities to them? What have you done so far to deal with the problems in each relationship? And what have you done so far to meet your responsibilities to each individual? Again, in the third area: What are the issues that have arisen?, What have you done about them?, and What do you want me to do about them? These three questions, in these three areas, quickly will uncover most relevant data initially needed for helping the counselee to meet the crisis.

And, may I point out in passing, that care in gathering data, plus homework based upon the data that are gathered, separately (or in conjunction) will expose which crises are real and which are imaginary; which are contrived and which are genuine. Stress upon feelings alone will never disclose such information; counseling that is abstract also will fail; it is only when we become concrete, ask for facts and take them seriously that the truth will come out. You cannot deal in facts for very long without discovering what you need to know about these matters. You can go on deceived for months, or even for years, if you fail to work with facts. This first activity, then, is foundational to all else. Do it well, if you wish the rest to proceed smoothly.

Secondly, having gathered whatever facts he can, the counselor will be concerned to reinterpret them for the counselee in biblical terms. I say reinterpret, not interpret. If the counselee had not put some interpretation upon the facts already, he would not yet knowingly be in crisis. And if he had not placed an erroneous interpretation upon the facts, the chances are that he would not be in need of counsel. We never take in data without placing some interpretation upon it; it cannot be learned apart from tagging it and responding to it. Language, in particular, becomes the vehicle for interpretation. So the counselor will be intensely interested not only in the basic thrust and import of the counselee's answers to his questions, he will be concerned also with particular words and phrases that most pointedly reveal the counselee's understanding and present stance toward the crisis. He will be most intensely interested in such telling words or phrases when they are repeated frequently. If the counselee continually says "I'm ruined!," or "It's too late!," or "What's the use of going on?," or makes any number of other such statements, the counselor knows that it will be necessary for him to reinterpret the situation in the light of the true, biblical import of the facts that he has gathered. As I have shown previously, when counselees speak of hopelessness and helplessness, it may be of importance to challenge this attitude by an exposition of I Corinthians 10:13, which then can be applied more specifically to the facts at hand." "Impossible," for instance, becomes "hard, but not too hard for God"; "out of control," becomes "difficult to control, but not out of God's control."

I wish to urge an important caution at this point. When reinterpreting, never so reinterpret a situation that in effect you *minimize* the severity of the problem. Take every problem most seriously, but insist that the counselee take God and His promises *just* as seriously.

The reinterpretation of facts can be all important. For instance, if a man who is a homosexual, looks on homosexuality as a sickness, the counselor will want to reinterpret the facts in biblical terms as *sin*. That can be crucial. If homosexuality is hereditary, or if it is a sickness, there is no hope for change. If it is sin, there is all the hope that there is in Jesus Christ. Labels, like "sickness" and "sin" are the results and signs of interpretations. But they are more than that; they also are *signposts* that point to solutions, or at least to the direction that one must turn to attempt to find a solution. "Heredity," for example, points not to Christ (He died, not to change our hereditary makeup, but for our sins.), but up a dead end street. (Who can get new parents and start all over again with a new sets of genes and chromosomes?) "Sickness" points to the physician; "sin" points to Christ.

Thirdly, in getting a grasp on the facts through analysis, the counselor will want to help the counselee to assess the facts. Here he is concerned to narrow the working field. Consequently, he will try to divide matters into separate categories, as for instance, questions of immediate concern ("How do we get Mary to unpack her bags and remain?," or "Is it really true that she is pregnant, or does she only *think* so?," or "You have got to put down the gun, John, so that we can talk about whether your life *is* worth living?"), and questions less pressing ("You can decide about selling the business and moving to another state at a later point," or "Let's schedule the discussion of what to do about your financial condition in general after we decide what to do about the one creditor who has been phoning you for a week").

Another way of assessing priorities is to ask "what are the *simple* issues and what are the more *complex* ones?" Often, as we saw in the last lecture, it is not so much a question of *what* a person does at the outset of a crisis as it is a matter of doing *something*. Simpler issues, usually, therefore, are to be preferred over more complex ones at such a time. John simply told Gaius, for the time being, to continue showing hospitality to the missionaries and to concentrate on doing it well. The more complex matters of Gaius' relationship to Diotrophes and to the church were left for later on. Closely related to distinguishing between simple and complex matters is the assessment of issues as having greater or lesser consequences. Again, it is wiser to begin with the latter.

Fourthly, in gathering, reinterpreting and assessing the facts, certain data will fall out as uncertain, tentative, possibly more matters of emotion than fact, conjecture and speculation, or even bizarre. This material must be sorted and sifted out from the working data. It should be rejected, deferred and shelved, or similarly disposed of whenever possible. If the data are basic or of central concern and cannot be separated from your approved accumulation, then they must be handled on the spot. But this is rare. Even when a dramatic matter like having hallucinations may *seem* to be a significant part of the problem, and when it deeply troubles the counselee, it is often possible to defer a full investigation and discussion of the question by observing that in many instances that are not drug related, hallucinations occur as a secondary complicating problem as the result of significant sleep loss. If it is at all likely that this is the situation, the matter of hallucinations should not occupy too much time and thus divert attention from the issues over which the sleep was lost. Simply put the counselee to bed!

Sorting out usable facts from questionable or unusable materials is an essential step to take before taking the fifth one. But, when you have sorted and sifted the wheat from the chaff, you have yet one vital matter to which to attend—the programming of the factual data that remain in the sieve for discussion, decision and action.

According to the interpretations and assessments made, these data must be scheduled in an order of priority for handling. Scheduling and priority setting are two activities that are absolutely essential for helping persons in crisis. Often, the counselee's judgment and sense of perspective is clouded or out of focus. He may tend to make decisions on the basis of feeling rather than out of conviction stemming from a prayerful consideration of the Scriptures. Unlike Moses, who traded the temporal riches of Egypt for the long term blessings of Christ, the person in crisis tends to confuse the short term with the long term. Often, simply scheduling matters of concern makes a significant difference. Getting it in order of priority, on paper, helps the counselee to see more clearly what is at stake. It gets him on track and keeps him there.

So, to conclude for today, remember, because the Christian counselor works with facts, he is concerned to analyze every crisis situation as fully as he can so that he may get a *grasp* on the facts about it. Getting such a *grasp* may involve five things:

G - Gathering facts

R - Reinterpreting facts

A - Assessing facts

S - Sorting or sifting out facts

P - Programming facts.

CHAPTER III

INVENTORY

"Do you always use mnemonic devices like AID and GRASP?" you may wonder. If you are not quite that kindly disposed, your question may take a slightly different form: "Really, don't you think that it's rather corny for you to pull something like this in a seminary context?"

Let me hasten to say that I would understand such a response. Indeed, I thought long and hard about doing this before I came. I knew that I might run the risk of turning some of you off. But, in spite of the dangers you can see that I opted for it anyway. "Why?" you ask. I'll tell you.

First, let me say that I don't do this often. Even a quick survey of my writings will prove that. So, why now? Because of our present subject matter. We are talking about *crisis* counseling. In a crisis everyone—even the counselor—needs firm structure. A crisis is a time when emotion runs high, and it is a time when the things that ordinarily you can depend upon to stay tacked down, come loose. It is easy not only for the counselee to be swept along by the emotion and the pressures of the moment—the same danger also exists for the counselor. It is all too easy for him to become confused about what his role may be, what he must do, what is to remain central and what is peripheral.

Therefore, any legitimate means that will help the counselor to remember what to do and how to do it in a crisis can be useful—even if it is corny. In fact, for mnemonic purposes, sometimes—the cornier the better!

The lifesaving people—to teach the types of water-rescue techniques available, and the order in which to use them—a few years back developed a little mnemonic. To many it might seem corny, but it proved its usefulness in saving lives. Here it is:

TOW/THROW/ROW/GO.

But notice, it was intended to help out in an emergency—in a crisis. *That* is when a firm structure for thought and action proves most useful. And—just by the way—before you gum that label "cornball" on me *too* quickly, let me remind you of a rather similar use of the mnemonic device, found in the *acrostic* Psalms! "O.K., O.K." you say. "If a mnemonic a day will keep confusion away, I'll try to stomach it. What's today's not-so-clever little piece? So far we've had A-I-D (Analysis, Inventory and Direction) and G-R-A-S-P (getting a grasp of the facts by Gathering facts, Reinterpreting facts, Assessing facts, Sorting out facts and Programming facts). Now, what about the I in Aid; how do we take an inventory of the person in crisis? Why don't you tell us right off today rather than keep us guessing?"

As a manner of fact, I think I shall. But, for variety's sake, I've changed my style. Taking the principle of "the cornier the better" seriously, today I have a poem for you. As I read it, see if you can spot the five key factors, in taking a personal inventory, of which this poem reminds you. Here is my little ditty. It is entitled,

"Inventory"

The counselee's *state*
may be sorry or great
Depending on what he has *done.*

If his *motives* are true
when he seeks help from you
Your battle's already half won.

What his *resources* are

will determine by far

If he'll lose or gain victory.

And through crisis he'll *grow*

if plainly you show

Opportunity through this [here] In-ven-tory.

All right; now that we've gotten past that, let's get down to business. In taking a personal inventory of the counselee, the first—and most obvious—place to begin is with the counselee's *state*. Remember,

The counselee's state
may be sorry or great.

Which is it? That is the first thing to determine. And it can be the all-important factor.

What I am referring to when I speak of taking an inventory of the counselee's state is asking questions like these:

1. *Is he in full possession of his faculties?* A drunk on the telephone threatening suicide is not. A counselee doped up by drugs (either self-administered or prescribed by a psychiatrist or physician) is not. A parent who is in shock after hearing of the sudden and unexpected death of his daughter less than fifteen minutes before is not. A counselee hallucinating as the result of significant sleep loss is not. These, and any number of other causes like them may lead to the judgment that no information, or only partial information may be obtained at present from the counselee himself. It may be necessary to gather data from other involved persons instead.

If the counselee is only confused or emotionally supercharged, heavy structure brought to bear on the situation by the counselor can make a great difference. If the counselor's own state is calm, cool and confident, if he exhibits a rock-ribbed faith in the promises of God, and if he communicates hope and order in the midst of chaos by the proper sort of take-charge manner, his modeling will exert a powerful influence upon the counselee. Remember the effect of Paul's manner during the storm at sea (Acts 27). In such instances, as a result, after a short time, the counselee himself may be in a position to cooperate fully with the counselor.

If, however, some of the more serious disorientations mentioned above seem to be present, another sort of action is called for. To keep him from injuring himself or others, the counselee may need to be placed under the supervision of someone until the effects of the disorienting factor wear off. He may need to be put to bed. Medical assistance at times may be required. In such cases, the counselor must postpone his offer of direct help in meeting the crisis in favor of ministering to the secondary needs of the person in crisis.

2. *Is he a Christian or non-Christian?* The counselee's state will be affected across the board by the fact, and the counselor's approach also will be affected at every point by the answer to this question. Paul wrote "we grieve (but) not as others who have no hope" (1 Thess. 4:13).

I cannot discuss the matter of evangelism in crisis here at any length. Let it suffice to say that after helping minimally at first in whatever ways that he can in order to eliminate distress, confusion, etc., the Christian counselor soon should seize the opportunity to disclose the true nature of the crisis—i.e., that the counselee is trying to understand and solve the problems of a sinful world without Jesus Christ. The approach will vary from person to person as it must in all effective evangelism—Jesus never evangelized the same way twice. The abrupt approach to Nicodemus contrasts dramatically with the slower and more gradual one used in speaking to the woman at the well recorded in the next chapter. Both differ strikingly from the account of the evangelization of the blind man in Chapter 9 of John's gospel. *There,* we learn that Christ did not even mention the way of salvation on the first encounter, but merely sent him to the pool of Siloam for healing. When interrogated about his remarkable recovery he could say no more than "This one thing I know: whereas once I was blind, now I can see!" It was only during a second encounter that Jesus spoke to him about the healing of the blindness within. In each case, the *approach* differed; in each, however, the purpose and the message were the same. As soon as it was appropriate the Lord introduced them to Himself as Savior.

The same basic approach to evangelism must be followed today. God, in His wise providence, sometimes brings about a crisis in order to cause the counselee to reconsider his ways. The counselor must be sensitive to the opportunity that ground well ploughed affords, and must sow the gospel seed. After all, every person who seeks counsel admits that he needs help. Evangelism is a matter of showing why.

3. *Is his attitude proper or improper?* If the counselee is bitter and resentful, or angry and sarcastic, or fearful and worried, it may be impossible to help him to discuss and to handle the issues involved in the crisis until the counselor has helped him to change his attitude. If he is guilty of having brought the crisis upon himself, that too may call for the counselor's immediate attention. Since I have said so much about how to handle these matters in other places, I shall spare you any repetition here. It is enough to point out that until he is right before God and his neighbors, all else that he may attempt will, judged by God's standards, fail.

Now, back to the poem:

The counselee's state

may be sorry or great

Depending on what he has *done*.

By this next line I am not speaking about what he may or may not have done to bring about the crisis. Rather, I am concerned about what he has done thus far *in response* to it. This, all-too-often neglected consideration can be critical.

Job's counselors put the emphasis upon responsibility for bringing about the crisis (as I noted in my first lecture) and thereby failed to help him since in reality he was struggling with the problem of how to understand it and what to do about it. Job's situation clearly parallels the one that I now have in mind.

If the fisherman tries to untie a knot in his line and, instead, succeeds only in putting six more knots in the monofilament, he has complicated the original problem by his faulty attempts to solve it.

That is the sort of thing that I had in view when I wrote "Depending on what he has *done.*"

Let us take, for example, a typical crisis. Mary has packed her bags; she plans to leave Tom the next day. He is afraid and desperate. Obviously, he does not know how to communicate with her or the marriage probably never would have reached this bitter point. But he loves her; he doesn't want her to leave. He pleads with her not to go; he begs her to give him another chance. Yet, as he promises her that he will "do anything" that she asks if only she will reconsider, by his tears and begging he succeeds in further knotting the line. One of the things that disgusts Mary is his weak unmanly ways. Here he is—acting like a snivelling animal—cringing at her feet. Failing in this sort of appeal, he is angered and begins to tell her so. His pride is injured; he has humiliated himself before her and has been rejected. He loses his head and tells her off; the venom he pours forth opens old wounds. He stoops even to name calling. More knots. When you see them for counseling, the original issues over which Mary decided to leave may be very remote in comparison to the sting of the recent tongue lashing that she most vividly recalls. To focus only (or even first) on those distant issues and to neglect the more recent injuries therefore would be a colossal mistake.

Possibly in another case the two problems are confused. Difficulty over problems at work involving interpersonal rivalries together with unconfessed guilt over an extra-marital sex affair may lead to a number of sleepless nights for Roger. When he comes he says that it is because he has been hallucinating. He and his wife Jean initially talk about two or three weeks of depression preceeding the onset of hallucinations, but only vaguely intimate that something at work was troubling Roger. Yet, what could problems at work have to do with something as strange as these hallucinations? They tell you nothing about sleep loss. Only when, by probing, you discover this missing piece to the puzzle can you begin to make the other pieces fit. What they consider the most serious problem, the hallucinations, turns out to be secondary; the hallucinations are the result of the sense of guilt.

In Roger's case, what he has done, namely losing sleep over his sin rather than confessing it in repentance, has tied *him* in knots.

Take one more example. Perhaps the counselee has seen another counselor first. If that counselor has filled his mind with blame-shifting excuses by saying that his greatest problem is his wife, and has advised getting a divorce, both notions must be dislodged before one can go further.

In any case, it is vital to investigate what the counselee has done. If he has become discouraged by failing in his attempts to solve his problems, that will be important to know—he will need to be given hope. If he has become wary of counselors because of unfortunate previous experiences, *that* could be critical. If he has done nothing, that could be the *most* crucial fact of all. So, never fail to take an inventory of the counselee's response to the crisis.

The poem reads:

> The counselee's *state*
>
> may be sorry or great
>
> Depending on what he has *done*.

But then it continues in these words:

> If his *motives* are true
>
> when he seeks help from you
>
> Your battle's already half won.

And it is!

Let's take a case. Bill has separated from Janet. She wants him back. When she comes for help the concluding words of her story are: "I'll do anything to get him back." A wary counselor will want to pick up those words and discuss them with her:

> "Janet, I'm glad that you want Bill back, but your motives concern me. When you say 'I'll do *anything* to get him back; you are not speaking as a Christian should. I think that we must consider your agenda first."

It would be important for him to stress the fact that a Christian should want to do anything— *that God says* . That addition is not just a pious platitude; it is an extremely practical principle that on the one hand, limits her options and, on the other sends her to the Scriptures to find out *what* God says to do. She discovers that she cannot lie to get him back; she must receive him only on the right basis, etc. Moreover, because of her strong motivation, the counselor will want to caution her:

> "Janet, if you put 'getting Bill back' first, you may get him but not on the right basis. In this crisis put pleasing Christ first—even before Bill— and whether you get him back or not, you will succeed in your major goal, and you will be blessed."

Motives are tricky. It is always wrong to make judgments about another's motives. The counselor, unlike God, can look only on the outward appearance. But, as in the case above, he can discuss the counselee's motivational comments with him. He should listen carefully for such comments. Apart from motivation-revealing comments, he must confine his counsel to the counselee's outward behavior.

Of course, the counselor can *ask* about motives: "What were you trying to accomplish when you called the police?" or "What made you think that life was not worth living?" Yet, since man's heart is deceitful, the counselor cannot always be sure of the answers that he receives. How can he be certain that he, along with others involved, is not being "used" or "manipulated" to achieve some purpose high on the list of the counselee's hidden agenda?

Well, the answer to that is simple: he can't! That is, he cannot be sure that he is getting a truthful account, right away. Should he be suspicious, doubt every word, take nothing for granted? If that is to be his attitude toward a counselee, would it not be better simply to start guessing from the outset rather than waste time in data gathering? Of course, that is where the logic of such an approach leads; and there are counselors who, because they hold that counselees either do not know or will not tell the truth, do just that. With a few supposed clues, from language, dreams and bodily action, in accordance with a prepackaged system they *guess* about his problems.

The Christian can do no such thing. He is bound to take the counselee seriously. In I Corinthians 13, Paul clearly says that love runs a risk. That risk includes the risk of being deceived, being used, and being manipulated. He writes "love . . . believes all things, hopes all things" (v. 7).

Does that mean that the Christian counselor must become a naive pushover? No, not at all. It does mean, however, that in love he will always give the benefit of any doubt. It means that he will not only teach the husbands and wives that he counsels to do so; it means that he will demonstrate the same attitude in his counseling of those same husbands and wives. But won't he be deceived? Yes and no. At times he will. But at times any counselor will, regardless of his theoretical base. Unlike the guessers, however, he will never be *self*-deceived.

But when a counselor takes a counselee seriously about his statements, two things happen:

1. Often, the counselee who might plan to deceive or misstate the truth, changes his approach. Belief out of love often breeds truth. Counselees have told me so.

2. But, secondly, suppose this doesn't happen; what then? The facts alone must drive the counselor to doubt. He questions the word of the counselee only when he can do nothing else. Well, won't he go on, and on, and on being deceived then? No. Since he is working with facts and commitment, the Christian counselor will *(more* rapidly than others) discover the truth. When he takes a counselee at his word, he follows up on that word asking for more and more facts, to get the whole story. It is difficult for most persons to deceive in detail. And, then, the counselor gives homework *based* upon the data that he has received. When the counselee balks, he will want to know why; when the homework cannot be done, he will investigate that. In a variety of ways, then, sooner than one may think, deception is usually discovered.

But to return to the original concern, remember, the counselee— even a Christian counselee—often will tend to become self-centered and humanistic in a crisis. His Christian value system may be set aside for whatever seems expedient. It is the Christian counselor's privilege and duty to stand by and point to the fact that Christ *is* in this crisis and that in *all* things—even in this crisis— *He* must have the preeminence.

Let's continue to consider our little five part ditty. So far we have suggested taking an inventory of the counselee's *state*, his *responses* to the crisis, and his *motives*. Next, we turn to the matter of *resources*. Upon what resources will he depend to meet the crisis? Does he know what they are and how to utilize them? As I read from the poem once more, listen particularly to the part about resources; it stresses a key consideration:

> The counselee's *state*
>
> > may be sorry or great
>
> Depending on what he has *done*.

> If his *motives* are true
>
> > when he seeks help from you
>
> Your battle's already half won.

> What his *resources* are
>
> > will determine by far
>
> If he'll lose or gain victory.

Many persons fail to meet crises adequately because they do not avail themselves of all of the resources that have been provided by God. This, also, is one of the major reasons why they lack hope. They see only what they can see of the crisis with their noses pressed hard against the wall; they fail to benefit from the viewpoint of another perspective outside of themseves.

The poem suggests that there are a number of God-given resources from which the counselee may draw help and hope to meet the crisis. Three of these are:

1. Personal resources

2. Family resources

3. Church resources

Under the heading of personal resources—i.e., those resources to which he can turn *on his own without involving other persons around him,* I would like to mention just two: the Word and the Spirit. In a crisis, a believer is driven first to God. Prayerfully, he asks God for wisdom, and then seeks it in His Word. He is strengthened—or as James put it—blessed by the Spirit in the obedient doing of whatever the Word requires (Jas. 1:25). A wise counselor will always point a counselee to the Scriptures. Here, in doing so, he will force him to begin his search for solutions—and not merely solutions— *God's* solutions. A person in a crisis, like Peter, is sinking because his eyes and his thoughts are centered on the storm. He needs to be directed instead to the Christ of the Scriptures in whom is the solution to every problem. So, in taking an inventory, the counselor will be very much concerned about whether or not the counselee is facing the problem, *Bible* in hand.

What of prayer? Whenever I read the answers to the three basic questions: What is your problem? What have you done about it? What do you want me to do about it?, I find that in a majority of cases, question number two is answered the same way by Christians: "I've prayed about it." Some, perhaps, answer that way to sound pious; the larger number have really prayed. But their problem persists (otherwise they would not need to seek my counsel). Why? Because rarely is prayer *alone* the solution to a problem. It is never—by itself—the solution when God, in His Word, has required action as well. One may not ask for his daily bread and then sit back and wait for it when the Bible says that if a man will not work, he should not eat. More often than not, prayer constitutes the background for the solution that comes through dependent obedience. We should pray for wisdom and depend upon the Spirit to provide that wisdom as we search for it in His Word. We should pray for strength and depend upon the Spirit to provide that strength as we obediently step out by faith to do whatever that Word says.

Of course, not all knowledge and wisdom must be sought out anew in a crisis. Christians often have learned truth and developed skills in the past, by their study and practice of the Word, that can be newly activated to meet the present situation. Other sins have been confessed in the past; and God and those involved have forgiven them. Why shouldn't the admitted adulterer now seek forgiveness again? Why does he think that this sin of adultery is beyond the pale of forgiveness from God, or his wife or his church? What he needs to learn from the Scriptures at this time is not how to seek forgiveness—that he knows—but rather the fact that he now can have it. The counselors accordingly, will read a passage like I Corinthians 6:9-11 that speaks so plainly of the forgiveness and cleansing of an adulterer by God. He will turn to II Corinthians 2:7-8 where Paul urges that a repentant excommunicate—one who was accused of incestuous adultery—be forgiven, comforted and received with a reaffirmation of love. What the Christian in crisis needs to learn in such cases, is not about repentance and confession of sin, but about forgiveness for *this* sin.

There are times when all that is needed to tip the scale toward the solution of a crisis is information. This was true of the Thessalonian church. Some of their members had died. Their loved ones were grieving, but added to their grief was an erroneous notion that they had picked up in some way—Paul didn't seem to know exactly how—that no Christian would die before Christ's second coming. When believing loved ones died, they were shattered, and were losing hope.

Hearing of the crisis nature of this double grief, Paul winged off a letter to set them straight: "I do not want you to be ignorant, brothers, about those who are asleep . . . ." Then, he tells them the truth. And at the end of that information he writes: "Comfort one another with these words." The answer to the crisis was information—accurate, truthful, detailed, dependable—as so often it is.

In Paul's case, he had given them the facts beforehand. Throughout his Thessalonian letters he makes a point of this; he says, for instance about another matter: "When we were with you, we kept telling you that you were going to suffer affliction" (I Thess. 3:4; cf. also II Thess. 3:10 and I Thess. 4:11). So Paul did not wait until the crisis had come; he anticipated as many crises as possible and in advance taught how to meet them. This crisis had come because they had forgotten his teaching, thereby leaving themselves open to distortions of the truth. When you take an airplane trip, you are told *beforehand* by the stewardess what to do if you should have a need to use the oxygen mask. A card in the pocket of the seat describes emergency procedures, and the stewardess is required by law to point out the location of all exits. All too frequently, counselors find that Christians have not been prepared *beforehand* by their pastors for the crises into which they will come. A significant portion of the Bible is preparatory. For instance, much of Daniel and all of Revelation can be understood as information given beforehand, in order to help those who must live through the events that are predicted, do so in a manner pleasing to God. These are not books designed to arouse speculation and dissension; they are handbooks for living through times of crisis.

But the counselee must be shown that these very personal resources that a man has—the Scriptures and the Spirit—also point him beyond himself. They stress the need of turning to others. The writer of Ecclesiastes rightly observes that two are better than one in a crisis and that a three stranded cord is not easily broken (cf. Ecc. 4:9-12). This truth needs to be emphasized.

A person in crisis who has turned to a counselor, has sensed already something of this need. And if the counselor is a Christian, and if his counsel is Christian, the counselee has made a good move. Yet it is not only to pastors—or other supposed professionals in counseling —that one should turn. Galatians 6:1, Colossians 3:16 and Romans 15:14 are but three of the many passages that indicate that every Christian has a ministry of counseling. Parents should counsel children, member should stimulate member (to love and to good works). The whole body of Christ must be made available to each member in his crisis.

To begin with, the counselor should urge members of the family to take seriously their scriptural obligations and responsibilities in the home. A husband must be guided to assume the role of loving leader in time of crisis as well as other times. Submissive helper, is what his spouse must become. Children must be shown that they are in trouble because they have failed to rely upon the resources that God has provided for them in their parents. Parents must be taught how to care for and discipline their children without exasperating them and provoking them to anger, so that they find parental resources readily accessible. The family is a critical unit in God's order of things, containing such powerful resources that any counselor who does not recognize and draw upon them is a failure and a fool.

But, perhaps even more to our shame, we have almost entirely failed to use the corporate and individual resources that God has provided in the church and in its leadership. A boy wanting to kick the drug habit should have dozens of doors thrown open wide to receive him during the difficult period of withdrawal. A family in financial trouble should receive help from the deacons rather than turning to state welfare. There is no problem that can arise in which other members of the body can be of no help if they truly weep with those who weep and rejoice with those who rejoice.

A most powerful passage, that applies quite directly to Christians meeting each other's needs, is found in Paul's words to Titus when he says:

> Let our people also learn to engage in good deeds to meet pressing needs, that they may not be unfruitful (Titus 3:14).[1]

The Church has not learned this; principally because it has not been *taught to* do so, or *how* to do so. If a crisis is not a "pressing need" what is it? That is from one side, as encapsulated a definition of a crisis as you may get. Not all pressing needs are of crisis proportions, of course, but everyone in a crisis has pressing needs. The wise counselor will be one who turns to the members of the body for help. He realizes that he alone cannot provide all of the help to meet every crisis. He must mobilize the entire body not only to pray—as important as that may be—but also to "engage in good deeds."

Long before a crisis arises, the wise pastor has been organizing his people for it. When the crisis comes, he does not need to scurry about finding out who can do what, if persuaded. He *knows* where to turn for what from whom.

And, in closing this section, let me remind you, that the counselor himself, by his knowledge of the Scriptures, by his conviction that

---

[1] In the Appendix there is a song written by Mrs. William Banks in response to a request that I made while lecturing at Capital Bible Seminary. I noted how Titus 3:14 almost rhymed and could readily be put to music and that I hoped someone would do so since it is an important text that needs to be stressed. The tune is contemporary and could be taught to young people as well as adults.

God's Word has the answers, and by his firm personal structure, becomes a needed steady influence upon the person in crisis. He must be a man with God's viewpoint—i.e., a man of strength and hope.

Speaking of hope, and of the biblical viewpoint that brings it, leads us to the last point in this lecture: opportunity for growth. The poem once more; this time in its entirety:

> The counselee's *state*
>> may be sorry or great
>
> Depending on what he has *done*.

> If his *motives* are true
>> when he seeks help from you
>
> Your battle's already half won.

> What his *resources* are
>> will determine by far
>
> If he'll lose or gain victory.

> And through crisis he'll *grow*
>> if plainly you show
>
> Opportunity through this [here] In-ven-tor-y.

That is the key. The crisis is not to defeat him; he is to defeat it. The counselee must be given a vision of overcoming evil with good, of turning tragedy into triumph. He must see that it is God's purpose to use crosses to lead to resurrections. When sin abounds—and we must be entirely realistic about the *abounding* nature of sin— nevertheless, the counselor must point out, grace even more abounds. There is a solution to every problem! But that is not all. It is a solution that is designed to lead one *beyond* the place where he was before the problem emerged. Though man was created lower than the angels, and by sin descended into a still lower position, Christ's redemption did not merely put man back again into his original condition; He has raised him far above the angels. It is *more* than redemption! In Christ, humanity has been raised far above every principality and power of the universe to the right hand of God! That is a super-redemptive salvation.

The counselor, therefore in every crisis must seek out the opportunity for growth, the road to triumph, and the way to demonstrate that grace more abounds. This super super-redemptive viewpoint, above all else, should provide the needed hope.

A crisis is a sanctification context. It provides the opportunity to examine the old ways and put off those that are displeasing to God, while discovering and seeking to pursue the new ones set forth by God.

In a true crisis old ways come loose; old patterns crumble. A crisis is a time when something new must happen ("I must go on alone without John since his death," "I must now face the future as a single unwed parent with a child," "The house was wiped out in a flood; what do we do now?"). It is because of the absolute necessity of newness that the opportunity for growth is afforded. "If there must be change," the counselor may observe, "then let's be sure that it is God's change that occurs." The crisis should be seen as a divine catalyst for good. Your inventory of the counselee should aim at discovering whether he has such a biblical viewpoint. If he does not, you must make every effort to help him to acquire it. That notion of crisis as divinely catalytic cuts straight across the pathways of confusion and despair. It is a challenge flung in the face of the crisis; in it is a hope larger, fuller and more solid than tragedy. That hope will not fail, for it is founded on the faithfulness of the heavenly Father. It grows tall from the soil of the super-redemptive message of the whole Bible. Job learned it at length: "the Lord blessed the latter days of Job more than his beginning," we read (Job 42:12). Joseph experienced it, and Jesus accomplished it!

So, in full face of the fury, a believer's heart can be calm, his pathway can be clear and his life can *sprout* with *good green growth*. That is how to help another to view a crisis.

Let me close, then, not with a final recitation of the poem—as you expected—but with a summary. First aid for crisis counselors requires an analysis of the situation. That analysis demands a grasp of the facts: gathering data, reinterpreting data, assessing data, sorting out data and programming data. It also requires an inventory of the person in crisis. Again, five elements stand out:

The counselee's state

The counselee's response

The counselee's motives

The counselee's resources, and

The counselee's growth.

If you can remain alert to these matters when helping persons in crisis, doubtless, your ministry will be a great blessing to many.

CHAPTER IV

DIRECTION

Today is my last opportunity to speak to you. While every aspect of crisis counseling is important, what I have to say *today* is *most* critical. If the rest has not been done properly, it will be difficult to do *this* well. But if *all* of the rest is done, and even if it is done *well*, unless this last element is achieved, everything else will have been done in vain. Yet right here is where so many counselors fail—either they do not know how to give direction to a person in crisis or they wonder whether they should.

It is necessary to analyze the crisis situation, discovering the true dimensions of the problem, learning how to recognize its parts and how to arrange them in logical segments of manageable size, and limiting it through understanding the place of Jesus Christ in the crisis. Gathering, reinterpreting, assessing, sorting and programming the facts are vital, preliminary steps, all of which have as *their* goal *doing* something about them. So analysis of the crisis is not an end in itself; analysis is done to provide the right sort of material, arranged according to biblical priorities, *for action*.

The same is true of the work of taking an Inventory.

A personal inventory of the counselee is taken to enable both the counselor and the counselee to understand his strengths and weaknesses, his fears and faith, his knowledge and ignorance, *in order to* help prepare him, and encourage him, and guide him in taking the actions that he must in order to meet the crisis God's way. That is why his state, his responses to the crisis thus far, his motives, his reliance upon resources, and his viewpoint toward the crisis as an opportunity for growth are all of significance to the counselor. He wants to know about these factors just as he wants to know about the situation, because he recognizes that *this* counselee with all of his peculiararities, must meet *this* crisis situation with all of its particular configurations.

Some may think that the rigidity of the structure that I have suggested for discovering facts about the situation and the person will tend to make a counselor advise every counselee in a stereotyped manner according to a canned and refrigerated, cut-and-dried pattern. But that sort of thing is precisely what I am trying to avoid. It is because I am concerned about the *uniqueness* of every counseling case, that I have spent time trying to make you fully concerned about the many sides of each. You will notice that G-R-A-S-P involves five factors of analysis and the poem entitled "Inventory" also contains five elements. Try as I may, I could reduce neither to a lesser number. The reason for a list of no less than ten items to check out in every crisis is to be sure that no essential ingredient may be by-passed. The rigid structure pertains only to rigidity in gathering *all* of the variables that lead to the final combination that one must face in helping someone in a crisis. It is a rigid stance *against* stereotyping.

The place to look for the sort of rigidity that leads to stereotyping is in *this* lecture not in the previous one—because this is the one that has to do with directions for decision and action. If here, I were to come up with five or more elements, watch out;—then you could be sure that the data gathered in analysis and through inventory are not being given their proper weight. Decisions and actions would be shaped instead, by a prefabricated plan, rather than by the Scriptures applied directly to the data at hand.

But I do not have a five item check list for direction in counseling; I have but three, and the third item is not always pertinent. The data in each case must determine whether or not this item is of significance.

My mnemonic today, then, is quite simple. We are concerned with issues. Remember, a crisis always raises one or more issues that demand a response. A crisis is a situation requiring change. Therefore *action* is the key to resolving a crisis—and, of course, the decision *not* to act, is itself an action of the most profound importance. Since *action* is at the heart of directing counselees how to handle issues, my three letter word today is A-C-T, ACT. These three letters stand for direction that is

Authoritative

Concrete

Tentative.

Analysis, Inventory and Direction; that is what the counselor must be prepared to bring to a crisis. Ability, knowledge, wisdom and courage in pursuing each of these activities is of utmost importance.

But before I speak of direction, let me discuss for a moment why direction is important. There are two basic reasons. First, when a crisis arises, it comes as a storm that foams up issues which demand decision and action. That demand puts the person in the crisis under pressure. That pressure comes from without but also triggers pressure from within. A person in a crisis—especially one who has asked for the help of a counselor—is *always* a person who is under heavy emotional pressure. His emotions are aroused for action. That is good and should give hope of effecting change quickly, but when emotion *prevails,* the logical side cannot always be depended upon to operate as efficiently as one might wish. Therefore, the presence of another, who is trusted and trustworthy, can be an important asset, since he stands at a greater emotional distance from the issue, and can make a less clouded assessment of it. Direction, then, is of importance even if it takes only the form of giving a second biblical opinion on the crisis.

There is, however, a second reason why direction is important. It is because, as I said before, action cannot be avoided. The crisis itself demands action; that, we saw, is inherent in the nature of a crisis. But now, I want to point out, that it is true that the *person* in crisis also demands action. It is the nature of a problem of crisis proportions that so excite the person involved that he becomes mobilized for action. If a person were not so intensely involved, he would not be in crisis. Nor, it should be observed, is it wrong (in itself) to allow one's self to be emotionally activated by a crisis. God made us that way. Stoicism, with its doctrine of the dispassionate disposition, is not Christian. Jesus wept. (Jn. 11:35), He cried down woes on the Scribes (Mt. 23), He turned on the Pharisees with anger (Mk. 3:5) and when He drove out the money changers, he cried

"Zeal for My Father's house has *eaten me up!*" All of that is evidence of strong emotion (much of it—incidentally—exhibited in crisis situations). So, I want to repeat, it is not wrong to become emotionally aroused over a crisis. That emotion leads to the mobilization of all of the bodily faculties. This mobilization and energizing of the body and mind occurs in order to prepare one to meet a difficult situation. That is good, not bad, *if* the energy is controlled by scriptural principles and focused biblically. Emotion becomes bad if, unharnassed, it takes over and gains control of the person. If there is doubt or uncertainty about the situation or about what God requires of the one who faces it, emotion is likely to take over. A "double minded man is unstable in all his ways" (Jas. 1:8). If, instead of welcoming the bodily tension, the counselee fears it and through that fear triggers additional anxiety, which causes more tension that he fears . . . and so on, the bodily stimulation can escalate out of control and the emotion that should act as a servant can become an unwelcome and terrifying master. Lastly, if energy that is mobilized for action is not put to work constructively doing those things that are required by God in His Word, that energy will be used destructively. The body will be injured internally, sleeplessness and anxiety may occur, and foolish and unwise decisions are likely to be made.

That is why directive counseling is so vital to a person in crisis. Rogerian, non-directive counseling, reveals its utter poverty, *perhaps most clearly,* when one uses it to try to help someone in a crisis.

When in a crisis, the counselee is reaching for the panic button, a wise directive counselor is always ready to point to other more advisable moves. He does not hesitate to show him other biblical buttons that he should push instead. Indeed, it is his task to uncover these buttons.

That is why direction is so vital in a crisis. The takeover of emotion narrows one's vision to a small unrealistic and unchristian band of possible actions ("I'll sell my house and move to Florida; I'll never be able to live alone," or "I can't face this; all I can do is lie about it"). A counselor can help broaden the band again, pointing to the true options set forth in the Scriptures. But one must *know* those options if he would be a faithful counselor.

Psychology does not prepare one to know Biblical answers. That is another reason why *Christian* counseling by pastors who know the Word in depth is essential.

Before I consider direction in its three dimensions, I should like to mention the importance of another element that is a part of all counseling that—in a crisis, especially—takes on particular significance. It is the importance of a personal presence. Both the word *paracaleo* and the word *noutheteo* speak of help from the outside. They picture the helper standing beside or in front of the counselee to assist, encourage and confront in whatever ways may be necessary. In some of the counseling situations to which I have referred thus far, that personal element is prominent. For instance, both in II John (written to warn against extending hospitality to false teachers) and III John (written to insist upon hospitality for true teachers in spite of a schizmatic condition in the congregation) John speaks of earnestly wishing to be *with* the reader that their joy may be full. He speaks (further) of making plans to do just that. In writing to the divided Philippian church about the need for unity, Paul twice refers to his absence in strong and moving words (1:27;2:12). There is no question about the fact that he would like to be present personally to resolve the issues. Like John, he recognized the desirability of having a counselor on hand to help those who are facing the crisis. Even though he himself could not be present, John sent Demetrius to help Gaius, and Paul did not merely *tell* Euodia and Syntache to be reconciled, he asked the pastor of the church to see to it that this reconciliation takes place.[1] Paul counted on the power of a personal presence.

What makes the presence of an outside party in a crisis important in all of these instances, is not merely the comfort and encouragement that he might offer. That, everyone knows about already, and so it goes without saying. There is another equally critical element in these biblical accounts that stands out: it is an emphasis upon the structure that these involved outsiders bring to those who, because of fear, weakness, lack of knowledge or confusion, so desperately need. When things are out of control—or are likely to get out of hand—someone present, who has deep concern, who knows and

[1] Philips 4:2,3. Cf. more detailed comments on this matter in Shepherding God's Flock, Vol. III, pp. 70-72.

loves the Word of God, and who can minister through bringing structured control to the person in crisis, is a valuable asset. Counselees often have expressed it this way:

"Thanks, not only for helping me to understand what God wants me to do, but also for insisting that I do it."

People—especially confused people in a crisis—know that they need such help.

All right. Now for A-C-T. Direction in counseling, first of all, must be *authoritative*. When a woman says "I want to divorce my husband," and you (as her counselor) know that she does not have biblical grounds for doing so, it is not enough to urge her to change her mind on principles of expediency. You do not ultimately argue that it will cause more harm than good, that the children will be adversely affected, etc.; instead you must go right to the heart of the issue and tell her: "You may not do so; it would be sin." And, you back up what you say with an exposition of the Word of God.

Authority in counseling, just like authority in preaching, is on two levels. There is the authority of the message and there is an authority of the messenger. The latter is a derived authority and stems primarily from his appointment as the message bearer. In the final analysis, it is the fact that one ministers God's Word that constitutes the fundamental element in his authority.

Since that is the case, it is essential to bring scriptural content to bear upon the crisis issues. The divorce question, mentioned above, can be settled authoritatively in no other way. The matter is not settled, however, merely by quoting a verse as if to do so has some magical power. Every verse used, unless entirely transparent to *both* parties, should be explained in terms of its contextual and grammatical import. The *telos,* or purpose, as well as the meaning of the passage, should be made crystal clear. Counselors must take the time to do so. It is only when a truth of the Bible is *understood,* and when it is *evident* that the Bible actually does teach that truth, that a believer comes under the full weight of its authority. Thus, in counseling, the truth of what the counselor says should be shown so plainly to be biblical that the counselee—even if he did not before—knows now what the verses that the counselor used mean, *and* what meaning they have for his situation.

The authority of the individual comes from the fact that he is true to the Book, resting all that he says upon its teaching and becoming a faithful and helpful interpreter for others. When in his life, he manifests the truth that he unfolds, that does not add authority to the message, it only adds authority to the messenger. It does do two other things, however. First, it keeps down any unnecessary confusion between the message that he speaks and the message that he lives. Secondly, harmony of message in word and life *demonstrates* the practicality and *possibility* of obedience to the counselee, and it shows him how to put it into effect. This affords great hope. It is confusing to insist on faith from others while showing no faith in them. It is difficult to understand truth abstractly without a model.

A faithful counselor will always distinguish between those truths about which he is sure and those about which he yet has some question. "I think . . ." will be reserved for the latter, while he will say clearly about the former "God says" or "the Bible teaches." Since the teacher of the Word shall incur stricter judgment (Jas. 3:1), the counselor will want to be very sure before he speaks with such finality. He does not want to be found misrepresenting God. But when he is sure, he can do no less than speak with authority.

He will be sure of his ground, as a result, and will prove a great blessing in crisis counseling, if he takes the time to study the Scriptures regularly, and labors long and hard over the difficult portions. A background in psychology, I think you can see, is not a background calculated to produce authority. For that, one must have a background in the Scriptures. Unless he has spent much time in preparation, thinking problems through in advance according to the biblical principles that apply, under the pressure of a crisis he will prove to be but a broken reed. It is in a crisis, when the tops of the trees are touching the ground, and when the shingles are coming off, that he must be a steady and sure influence. But he will be like a house built on the rock *only* if he *hears* Christ's Words and *does* them.

When everything else is coming apart, the person in crisis wants to know what it is that is immovable. He wants a solid place to plant his feet firmly. The counselor who can point him to the appropriate portions of the "Word of our God" that "stands forever" (Isa. 40:8) will bring the help that he needs most. Authority in a crisis is the most vital factor of all; without it, all that is done is but speculation and guesswork.

Since people seem to find it difficult to distinguish between things that differ, let me say just a word about the difference between authority and authoritarianism. There is a difference, you know. Authority (for the Christian) is found in words and acts that come from God. The emphasis in such authority, as I have said, is not upon the messenger but upon his message. That is to say, authority, rightly exercised, points one to God who is *the* Authority. Authoritarianism, on the contrary, points away from God and, instead, focuses upon the messenger. His manner, his position, etc. become the most vital facts. It is so bad a distortion of authority that the divine message is made to exist for the sake of the human messenger. Far from confusing the two, you must see, rather, that they differ so greatly that, in fact, they are opposites.

We shall turn now from a discussion of the need for biblical authority in decision making and action to a brief consideration of the "C" in A-C-T, concreteness. Directive counseling must be concrete.

If direction is the place in which counseling founders, we shall see that it is in these waters also that she most frequently shatters her hull and sinks. In counseling and in preaching, in general, the tendency is to be general and abstract. Why? There are probably a *number* of reasons for this, but let me suggest only two. First, much of the material that pastors read is abstract. In their preaching and in their counseling, they tend to reproduce what they consume.[2] At our counseling center, as I observe our trainees, this seems to be their No. 1 problem. It most readily can be detected in their language, which is often technical. Jargon, peculiar to theologicans, never should be used in counseling, unless *absolutely* necessary—and then, only in connection with careful explanation. And, when counseling in a crisis, you can see readily how such language could get in the way. Why create new and artificial problems for the counselee by talking about soteriology when you can say salvation, or the noetic effects of sin when you can talk about the way sin has

---

[2]That is one reason why pastors should make it a habit to read books other than theological ones.

affected thinking? Worse still is when ministers try to bolster their counseling with a sprinkling of psychological jargon. Not only is this inappropriate, but usually these terms are used imprecisely and with confusing results. How often have I heard a minster speak of someone having a "guilt complex," when really all that he meant was that the individual had a sense of guilt. The first expression is fuzzy and confusing; the second sharp and clean. Words like neurosis, schizophrenia and paranoia are especially bad since the words themselves have become imprecise. The word "schizophrenia," for instance, has come to mean nothing more than bizarre behavior. Like the words "red nose," it speaks *only* of effects, not of causes. You can get a red nose by falling asleep under the sun lamp, growing a pimple on it, getting punched in it, or, I suppose, in at least a hundred other ways. The same is true of bizarre behavior—it may come from significant sleep loss, the ingestion of LSD, a desire to deceive, malfunction of bodily chemistry, or who knows what? Moreover, the use of such terms points in the wrong direction. They are associated with psychiatry and therefore point to supposed psychiatric solutions, whereas terms like sin, point to Jesus Christ.

But secondly, abstract concepts, language and discussion may grow out of fear. To keep a discussion either in the pulpit or in a counseling session in the realm of the abstract of course is the *safest* thing to do. You have run no risk of contradiction or argument when you tell him that he must "become more loving" toward his wife. The word love (when so used) is an abstraction, about which you and he can talk forever, and yet see no change. He can protest till the cows come home that he is "trying to be more loving," and that his wife is "an insensitive person" who just doesn't appreciate his attempts, and there is no way for you or for her to prove him wrong or right. But, if the words *love* and *insensitive* are concretized; i.e., spelled out in terms of what, specifically, they mean in this marriage, *then* there can be a monitoring of the progress of both the husband and wife. If his attempt at showing love, for instance, is first spelled out as doing one new small thing for his wife each day for a week—just to please her—and if being sensitive to his efforts is delineated as being aware of and expressing appreciation for each attempt by taking note of it and saying "thank you," then the progress or lack of it can be pinned down.

It is upon this aspect of concreteness that I wish you would focus your attention for a few more minutes. People do not change in the abstract; they change only in doing concrete things. An inconsiderate person cannot work on becoming considerate. Inconsideration and consideration are mere abstractions; they are simply words that should head columns of acts that a person does or doesn't do. A husband can't work on being considerate, but he can put his socks in the hamper each day instead of throwing them on the floor and expecting his wife to pick them up. She can screw the top back on the toothpaste tube instead of leaving it off when she has finished with it. Life consists of thousands of small things, like these, that—in and of themselves—are not very important. But when changes are made even in such small annoying patterns as these, especially if they have persisted over a considerable period of time, others can *see* that love, or concern, or considerateness is being expressed. Big changes in relationships can result from small changes in practice.

It is right here that a crisis counselor must excel. Since a crisis, by definition, is a situation requiring a change, the Christian counselor must know how to use the Scriptures in a thoroughly concrete manner. He must learn how to apply biblical truth specifically to given situations in a way that makes it plain to everyone what God requires. He must not speak in platitudes; he must work at the level where the rubber meets the road.

For example, if a husband has been caught in adultery and says that he wants to repent and rebuild his marriage, it is not enough to talk about those matters in the abstract. The counselor will want to make sure that both parties understand the nature of repentance, that forgiveness is sought and granted not only from God, but also from his wife. He will be deeply concerned that she understands forgiveness as a *promise* to remember his sin against her no more. In accordance, he will show how she must not bring the matter up again to him, to others, or to herself. It is the last point that is so difficult: how to keep from dwelling on it and, as a result, feeling sorry for herself and angry toward him. The counselor will help her to work on this *concretely,* perhaps he will suggest that she keep a tight schedule, allowing little or no time for wool gathering, that she develop a Philippians 4 *think list* of profitable mind-engaging subjects to carry about for use at times when she is tempted to sit and soliloquize. Instead, she can whip out her list, turn to the next item

("Planning menus for our family campout") and go to work on it.[3] For his part, the husband's repentance will be accepted concretely: "If, as you say, Bill, you want to rebuild your marriage on an entirely new basis, let's get to work on that right away. First, this week, you and Phyllis make a list of at least 50-100 concrete ways in which the marriage should change.[4] Next week we shall begin to work on these, one by one." When people came to John the Baptist and asked "What shall we do?," he told the tax collectors to stop stealing, the soldiers to put an end to the abuse of their power, etc. So too, modern counselors must be concrete; repentance should be followed by the specific "fruit (or change) that is appropriate to that repentance." The Christian counselor, in such situations, not only must *know how* but also must *show how* to make the changes that repentance requires.

One of the chief reasons people go to counselors is to learn the *how to*. For years they have heard the *what to* from pulpits ("study, don't merely read your Bibles," etc., etc., etc.) in a well-meant but abstract fashion. Now they want to know how to do it. Any counselor who does not wish to or does not know how to give instruction in the how to, will fail. Mark that down as a fact. The how to is simply the application of scriptural truth to specific situations. But that is the hardest, most painstaking part of counseling. Because it is so difficult, many counselors shy away from it. Yet, for this reason—because of its difficulty—it is preciseley here that counselees need help most desperately. Abstracting the principles that apply to a counselee's situation is helpful. But then abandoning the counselee at the very point where those principles can begin to change life, is both cruel and counter productive to all the good that otherwise might have been accomplished. Yet, so often this is exactly what is done. As a result, all of the previous work that may have been accomplished is lost, and all of the hopes that have arisen, evaporate.

I do not wish to suggest that the counselor must make every application of every principle to every item on the counselee's list;

---

[3] The first item on the think list which I always give the counselee as a starter is: "Items for my think list."

[4] 50-100 items will assure you of a list that is concrete. People cannot think of that many options. It will also make it clear that you expect hard work.

that would be too much for him, and ultimately it would not help the counselee. But he must help him sufficiently enough to do at least three things: (1) change the situation markedly so that he begins to get a taste of what biblical living can be like, (2) turn things around enough to get him heading at last in the right direction and (3) demonstrate fully enough how to apply the Scriptures to concrete problems that the counselee himself now knows how to do so and is, indeed, both *willing and able* to do so himself. The remaining work, then, and only then, can be safely left for the counselee to accomplish on his own.

Now, for the T in A-C-T, Tentative. Direction, in and during the crisis period, often must be tentative. What is done will be preparatory, partial or provisional. More often than not, what is done will constitute but a beginning. A calmer, more relaxed sort of counseling may then take up where crisis counseling leaves off. Since one of the chief goals of crisis counseling is to extract the emergency factor, thereby removing a good bit of pressure from the situation and deflating it from its crisis proportions, the *focus* of crisis counseling will be narrower than that of ordinary pastoral counseling. This more limited concern is reflected in what I have called tentativeness in providing direction.

Three things may be said about the tentative approach in giving direction:

1. Some directions must be *preliminary*. If, for instance, in taking the counselee's inventory, you discover that his *state* is not conducive to counseling or decision-making, you must take preliminary measures to meet the situation. If he has taken an O.D. (over dose), hospitalization probably will be required. If he is drunk, first, he must be sobered up. If he is perceptually unstable from sleep loss, a sleep binge of two days may be the most important direction that can be given. In the case of a husband and wife who are on the verge of separation, you may need to spend all of your first session persuading her to unpack her bags. But because you did not have time to do more, you will want to set up some early walk-on-eggs measures to help them to get through those next two days until you can see them again. Before all of the data can be *grasped* or the full *inventory* of both parties can be taken, and more concrete direction

can be given, you want to try to avoid any more complications, so you may give a preliminary direction like this:

> "Between now and when I see you next, I want you to do three things. First, ask God to help you to hold your tongues. Secondly, whenever anything goes wrong, instead of trying to settle it yourselves—we haven't had a chance to work on how to settle differences God's way yet—on this pad of paper write down what went wrong and bring it with you the next time. Thirdly, read this book—especially noting the chapter entitled "Communication Comes First," and we shall begin to get into these matters in more detail next time."

Obviously, those directions are not optimal, but sometimes—when all of your time has been spent on getting a preliminary agreement not to leave, or on seeking agreement to let you help before taking some radical step, that is all the direction that you can give. But keep in mind, *some* direction is necessary—even if it *is* preliminary. Persons, highly motivated for action, must be given something to do. Otherwise they will do something—usually the wrong thing—anyway.

2. Some directions must be *postponed.* Whenever it is possible to put off certain decisions or actions, it is desirable to do so. Hasty decisions about large matters, always ought to be postponed until the crisis is past. The widow who has just lost her husband is in no condition now to decide to sell the business, or to move to Florida, etc. She must be counseled to postpone any such decision until later, when she can amass the facts, more calmly assess them and can make the decision in full possession of all of her faculties. You must help her to sort out the crisis issues (i.e., what must be done *now*), from other issues. Thus, she must be taught the value of having a full grasp of the situation, and an awareness of her own state before moving ahead.

3. The counselor may promise to help his counselee to face the non-crisis issues at length, and (if he has learned how to sort out, assess and program the facts of the crisis situation) he can lay out a plan for handling them in a reasonable order, *after* the more immediate and more pressing demands of the situation have been met. All of which is to say that:

Some directions must be *preparatory*. Since a counselee who is motivated and mobilized to meet a crisis will want to expend his energy by *doing something*, I have noted that the counselor must put him to work in some way. Usually, the most productive way in which to do this is to find legitimate preparatory work for him to do. The idea is not to find busy work for him to do—although that often would be preferable to some of the actions that counselees propose—but rather *legitimate* work; i.e., work that (while preparatory, to be sure) nevertheless is work that will lead to a biblical disposition of the issues at hand. Preparatory work is action at least one step removed from final action. It involves activity that does not immediately commit one, can be changed if necessary and (when handled properly by the counselor who proposed it) has good, not evil consequences.

As far as possible, all short term work should relate to long term objectives; that is the rationale for calling it preparatory. Lists and schedules often provide the best sorts of preparatory work. By then, more data can be gathered, data can be classified and plans can be sketched. Writing out one's ideas helps him to clarify them and helps the counselor to see more exactly what he is thinking. The preparation of lists is preparatory to the actions implied or proposed in them. The counselor can discuss the lists with the counselee at subsequent meetings and they can be modified prior to action. Here, for instance, are some examples of lists that might be made:

1. List all of the problems that you see on the horizon.

2. List everything that will be affected by the change, and how.

3. List all of the decisions that you think you will have to make in the next three months. Divide these into two columns: (1) those I must make right away; (2) those I can postpone for a time.

4. List the exact process of events that took place in leading to this crisis.

5. List the names of all who are affected by this crisis and state how.

6. List your responsibilities in this crisis: what they are, to whom you are responsible and what God wants you to do to discharge them.

Preparatory action brings satisfaction and relief because it takes the pressure off, begins to sort out aspects of the problem and is a way of getting a toehold on the crisis. As he prepares, and as you help him to do so, the counselee will begin to discover God's way out of the crisis. I did not list Bible study or prayer in the six examples above, because I assume all along that these will play a significant part in the counselee's preparation. Mostly, he will need direct help in this before, during and after the preparatory work.

Well, there it is. For four days we have discussed—in a very spotty and preliminary fashion, an approach to crisis counseling. If you are dissatisfied, so am I. In four days we could only take a brief look at this critical subject. But I hope the dissatisfaction is not a dissatisfaction of disgust, but the sort of dissatisfaction that makes you determined to know more. I trust you will want to fill out the mere suggestions, illustrate and concretize my abstractions, and modify and adapt wherever your situation makes that necessary. But I hope that you will not want to leave and forget the whole business.

Of course, that's not really possible anyway. You may forget crisis counseling for a time. Indeed, you may even get along well in your pastorate without a thought of it—until one day at two A.M. when a drunken member of your congregation phones and on the other end of the line you hear these words:

"Pastor, I've got a gun at my head and if you don't tell me what to do, I'm gonna' pull the trigger."

What will you say? God help you if you don't know and God help that member.

EXPLANATION

In order to enable the reader to make immediate application of the biblical principles of Crisis Counseling that I have set forth in this book, I have added the ten sample cases in the following section. Each case involves a different sort of crisis that a pastor may be called upon to face.

By reading[1], discussing, practicing, role playing and evaluating each it is my hope that students (individually or in groups[2]) will learn how to *apply* crisis theory in a practical way. Those using or teaching these cases may wish to keep the following suggestions about role play in mind:

1. During group preparation of a role play for presentation it is most beneficial for each person in the group to take a turn playing the role of counselor.

2. It is perfectly all right to add any details to a case so long as it retains (1) the central problems indicated, (2) its crisis nature.

3. Role plays of counseling sessions should be condensed into fifteen minute periods (or less) to allow time for discussion and evaluation. Players should focus upon highlights and *necessary* details rather than taking time to relate all of the steps in the counseling process.

4. The fifteen minute segment should be followed by at least a fifteen minute analysis, evaluation and critique by the teacher and/or the

---

[1]As a background for general counseling principles (and for reference), consult (especially) my earlier books: *Competent to Counsel, The Christian Counselor's Manual, The Use of the Scriptures in Counseling* and *Shepherding God's Flock,* Vol. II.

[2]In class, at ministerial meetings, etc.

class, stressing apparent strengths and weaknesses and adding suggestions for improvement.

5. Remember that condensing inevitably leads to a more compact and therefore abrupt and slightly unnatural approximation of the real life counseling situation. Make allowances for this in evaluation.

The questions following each case are suggestive and are aimed principally at helping the reader to orient his thinking in a preparatory way about his task in each crisis situation. Space has been provided for notations following each question. Directions for role playing also accompany each case.

CONTENTS

CRISIS CASE #1

THE DEFORMED CHILD

Picking up the phone you hear a voice urgently pleading "Pastor, you'd better come over here to the hospital right away. We need you. The baby has just been born. Alice is O.K. physically, but the baby isn't —he—he has some terrible deformities. They say he'll never be right. The doctor told Alice about twenty minutes ago and she became hysterical. Nobody here can seem to quiet her. Please come; maybe you can help."

Cliff and his wife Alice are members of your church. This is their first child. Both have seemed to be very stable people.

Using the information in the preceeding lectures determine the answers to the following questions:

1. What do you know already, before going to the hospital?

2. On your way to the hospital, you try to think through the major objectives that you will try to reach. What are they?

3. From the list of objectives, formulate a plan of action by which you may structure your visit at the hospital. Set forth this plan by steps.

Role Play: From these conclusions, enact the confrontation at the hospital.

CRISIS CASE #2

"HER BAGS ARE PACKED"

Pastor, I'm so glad you're here!" Martin blurts out as he rushes through the front door of your study. "Martha is outside in the car and she refuses to come in . . . but she says that she'll talk to you. You will talk to her, won't you?"

"Martin, please get hold of yourself," you reply. "Try to tell me what's happened, you are not making much sense."

"Well, pastor, she says she's leaving me. Her bags are packed and in the car trunk. I only convinced her to stop by here at the last minute. She was heading for the train station. She says that she'll listen to you, but that what you say had better be good, because unless it is, she's going and I'll never see her again. Pastor, please help. Please don't let me down. I love her. I don't want her to leave. Please talk to her—everything now depends on you!"

Questions:

1. What will you say to Martin immediately?

2. What will you try to get Martha to do?

3 How will you attempt to achieve this?

Role Play: Have the narrator relate the details as given above. Role play the counselor's response to Martin and his subsequent encounter with Martha.

CRISIS CASE #3

"I'M NOTHING BUT A MILLSTONE"

. . . "So that's why I called you and asked you to come," says Bart as he concludes a tale of utter defeat, failure and sin. "There is no use to try to go on. Everything I do is a failure; my wife and my children would be better off without me. I'm nothing but a millstone around their neck. I can't keep a job, I'm drunk half the time, and when I'm sober I'm so worried about the bills that have piled up and what I am doing to the family, that I'm not worth anything even then. Unless you can show me that there is some way out of this mess, I've decided to end it all. This bottle of pills will do the trick quickly and painlessly."

1. How will you respond to Bart?

2. What will your immediate objectives be?

3. What will you try to do next?

Role Play: Act out two or three possible approaches to this situation. Try to stress the essential elements that must be included in any approach.

CRISIS CASE #4

"YOU TELL HER, PASTOR" . . .

Crushed, Mike did not know what to do. Nor did he know how to break the news. So he called you. You came. He asked you to remain and tell Brenda. As soon as she regained full consciousness you told her. Her words that follow are the climax of her response.

"But Pastor, I don't want to die! I'm only 43 years old! My husband needs me, the children are not yet raised and . . . Oh . . . Oh . . . Oh . . . What will I do?"

Brenda breaks into uncontrollable sobbing and buries her face in the pillow of the hospital bed. Not many hours before, her husband Mike had rushed her to the hospital for what seemed to be a serious, but (nonetheless) routine appendectomy. When the surgeon emerged from the operating room, he told Mike that he had found more than they had bargained for—there was cancer everywhere. He suggested also that from the looks of things Brenda might not live much longer. That was when Mike called you.

Questions

1. What is happening here?

2. Was this the time and place to tell Brenda?

3. What can you do to help her and Mike, now/later?

Role Play: Take it from the top, starting with Mike's phone call and moving beyond the point reached in the description above. Show how a Christian counselor might handle this situation. If you wish to change anything in the sequence of events as they are described, please do so.

CRISIS CASE #5

"A DIRTY LITTLE SLUT"

"But you did, you did!" screamed her mother; "you've lied and deceived us . . . and now see what it has led to!"

"You're mother's right" said her father angrily, "you are nothing but a dirty little slut! Think of it, pastor; she told us five months ago that she would never see that punk again, and now we not only find out that she's been sneaking out to see him, but to top it all off, as a result she's pregnant. What are we going to do?"

You reply "I know that both of you are angry, hurt and deeply disappointed, but . . . "

1. What will you say next?

2. How would you best be able to help the members of this family?

Role Play: Follow the format above and proceed from there.

CRISIS CASE #6

"I'LL KILL HER!"

"How can he do this to me? I've given him the best years of my life! I mothered his children, raised them all through thick and thin, and now—when the last one has just gone off to college—now when I thought that the two of us really could start to enjoy each other again with a new freedom, he tells me this! Think of it! He says I'm boring and dull and that he plans to run off with another woman. I'll kill her if he does; I'll kill that house-breaking hussy! I'll kill him too! Oh, pastor, what will I do? I love him. I don't want to lose him. I can't go on without him. Why did God let this happen? Can you do something to stop him?"

Marge has just finished telling you her story in a state of uncontrollably mixed emotions. She sits there in your study waiting for an answer. You are shocked. You had no inkling of a problem in this home. You can hardly believe your ears. Curt, her husband, is the Church School superintendent and Marge, a faithful leader of Pioneer Girls. "Could this really be happening to them?," you wonder.

1. Given your state and hers, what can you best do at the moment?

2. Later on?

Role Play: You may want to describe more than one counseling session in this role play.

CRISIS CASE #7

"WON'T TALK, EAT, MOVE"

She's been that way for hours, pastor. We don't know what's wrong, and we don't know what to do about it. She just sits there and stares; won't talk, won't eat, won't move. As I said before, all we know is that when she got that phone call, she cried out "O my God, no!" and sat down. There was no one on the phone when we got around to hanging up the receiver. Can you help us?"

1. Can you? If so, how?

2. If not, why not?

Role Play: Show clearly what you will do and say in this situation.

CRISIS CASE #8

SELL AND MOVE?

"He was buried only last week, but already I'm so lonesome and I miss him so much that I . . . " (Millie, the 73 year old widow of an elder of your church whose funeral you conducted breaks up in tears. After a time she continues:) "It's the hollow ring of the house. I forget for a moment and call to him and then I remember that there will be no answer. I sit at our table . . . alone. I sleep in our bed . . . alone. There is too much about this place that reminds me of him. Already I can see that I'd probably be better to get out of here. I've had a couple of real estate people call and ask about selling. I was wondering if I'd like it in Florida. What do you think pastor?"

1. Well, she's asked for advice; What will you tell her and how will you back it up scripturally?

2. How can you best protect and guide Millie at this time?

Role Play: Millie has tossed the ball to you; What will you do with it?

CRISIS CASE #9

A PROPOSITION?

Passing by the men's room in the far corner of the all-but-empty church basement after the evening service you are brought to a halt by the sound of two voices that are all too audible:

"No, I won't do it again. I'm tired of it. I'm trying to quit. It's sin and I know that the Lord doesn't want me to go on."

"But Harry, I've told you before . . . It's not sin when two persons are in love with each other as we are. Please, just once more. Just *this* time . . . . "

Can this be what it sounds like? And can that be Harry, your organist, and Jerry, one of your deacons? Well, it sure seems so. Then, what do you do next? Later?

Role Play: The next move is yours, pastor. What will you do? Show us.

CRISIS CASE #10

ONLY KIDDING

"Pastor, I appreciate the fact that you were willing to come over right away when it was so late." So speaks Nell as she opens the conversation. Her husband, Stanley, a long time member of the congregation is uncomfortably slumped down into the corner of the sofa, stone silent. She continues: "I wouldn't have dreamed of calling you under any circumstances unless it was serious. But this .. this is too much!"

"Oh Nell, I told you —you're making too much out of it. Getting the pastor out of bed and all of that, why—"

"Too much out of it! How can you say that, Stanley? Pastor, do you know what he proposed to me no more than an hour ago? He asked me if I'd be willing to participate in a swinging party this weekend. He wants to swap me off to another man so he can have sex with his wife!"

"I was only kidding. I told you that . . . !"

"Kidding? People don't kid about those things. Besides, I know you—I know you weren't kidding. You had that gleam in your eye— the same one you get whenever you see a pretty face and a sexy figure."

"Have it your way then . . . . "

And so it goes. Now, Pastor, they turn to you. What will you do?

Role Play: Be sure that you try to develop the crisis nature of the situation adequately and how you would seek to relieve it.